How to Pass Exams

Dominic O'Brien

How to Pass Exams

accelerate learning

memorize key facts

revise effectively

Foreword by Tony Buzan

WATKINS
Sharing Wisdom Since
1893

How to Pass Exams
Dominic O'Brien

This edition first published in the UK and USA in 2015 by
Watkins, an imprint of Watkins Media Limited
19 Cecil Court
London WC2N 4EZ

enquiries@watkinspublishing.co.uk

First published in the UK in 1995 by
HEADLINE BOOK PUBLISHING

Managing editor: Kelly Thompson
Editor: Hanna Bolus
Editorial assistance: Katie John with Kirty Topiwala
Designer: Suzanne Tuhrim with Allan Sommerville

A CIP record for this book is available from the British Library.

ISBN: 978-1-84483-391-7

10 9 8 7 6 5 4

Typeset in Minion
Printed in Europe

www.watkinspublishing.com

Contents

Foreword

Dominic O'Brien has now become globally known for his extraordinary mental powers. I had the privilege of first meeting Dominic in the late 1980s when I was in the process of organising the inaugural World Memory Championships. He told me that, like many students, he had been criticised in school for inattentiveness, daydreaming and for not being as interested as he should have been in the topics in the standard curriculum. Dominic's interests were more involved in the worlds of the imagination, music and developing his more general mental skills. As a result, he left school and began to study the art of memory.

Within five short years he had developed a gigantic "Memory Muscle" and was ready to challenge all comers at the first World Memory Championships in 1991. Taking on such legends of the mind as Creighton Carvello, who had set the world record for memorisation of the numbers of *pi* at 20,013 digits, Dominic virtually cruised to victory, clinching the title of first World Memory Champion and in the process breaking and setting mental world records.

Since then he has gone on to defend his title successfully and to establish a growing number of mental records, including the memorisation of a pack of cards in under forty-five seconds. Ranked No. 1 in the world in *Buzan's Book of Genius* (published 1994), Dominic is universally recognised as one of the greatest mental athletes in the world. After having seen Dominic smash world records with apparent ease in 1993 and 1994, Grandmaster Raymond Keene O.B.E., an authority on mind sports and chess, and chess correspondent of *The Times* and the *Spectator*, said that he had never seen anything so dominantly brilliant in the field of mental athletics.

What is more important for all students to realise is that Dominic achieved his extraordinary accomplishments by studying the field, by applying himself totally to the task he had set himself and by developing the natural skills which we all have.

In this excellent book on how to pass exams which you are about to read, Dominic reveals the methods and secrets by which he has achieved such enviable success. I recommend this book with delight, in the belief that all students will benefit from its clear advice, and look forward to seeing you challenge Dominic at the next World Memory Championships!

TONY BUZAN

1   Introduction

LEARNING HOW TO LEARN

Some years ago I watched an event that was to change my life. Creighton Carvello, a psychiatric nurse from Middlesbrough in the northeast of England, memorised the order of a pack of playing cards in just under three minutes. In doing so he achieved a new world memory record. So astonished and bewildered was I by this incredible feat of brain power that I began to investigate my own memory.

The burning question to me was whether Creighton possessed extraordinary powers of recall, or was privy to special techniques that could be used by the rest of us to train our own brains, producing equally stunning results.

After many years of intensive study in memory training, I am utterly convinced that most of us are quite capable of storing in our brain not just the order of a pack of fifty-two playing cards, but information in encyclopaedic quantities. The only thing preventing us from doing so is ignorance of the techniques and systems that would enable us to unleash the full potential of this remarkable resource – the brain –

which for most of the time lies unused within our skulls.

The key to memory development, accelerated learning and, ultimately, the passing of exams lies in our imagination. This book will show you how to unlock your own imagination by treating it like a muscle, and giving it regular exercise as it takes adventurous walks through familiar locations. You will discover how dull, unintelligible data can be converted into meaningful, memorable images by learning the colourful language of numbers. I will show you how historical dates, chemical symbols, foreign words and lines from literature can all be stored using three-dimensional mental filing systems. I will demonstrate how success can be achieved in academic disciplines as diverse as maths and media studies by simply using your memory to its maximum natural potential. By bringing the full capability of your memory into play and combining it with the most effective reading and revising techniques – both of which this book will show you – you will be well on the way to passing your exams with flying colours. No matter what your level of study – GCSE, A-Level, baccalaureate, B-Tec or Degree – if your course involves exams, your first steps to success lie here.

What a pity I wasn't shown these methods when I was at school, struggling away.

Belief and confidence
The root of my problems at school lay in a common, and misguided, belief. The belief that everyone falls into one of

two camps – that a child is born either with or without the gift of learning. Born to be scholarly or not. In short – bright or dim.

According to this belief, if you are unlucky enough to fall into the latter group, then you are destined to struggle and ultimately fail. At school I knew my place. I accepted my category. Just imagine what that did for my confidence!

What appeared to be a lack of concentration in class was in fact day-dreaming – one talent I did possess was an active imagination. What a tragedy this wasn't nurtured from an early age. For imagination, as you will discover, is the key to developing a perfect memory.

Learning how to learn

I hope your educational experiences haven't been as bad as mine were – I hated school. I accepted, reluctantly, that this was the way things were, but couldn't understand why I should be restricted to a watered-down, grey, overcomplicated, artificial, classroom version of the universe, when outside I could see life itself beckoning in all its three-dimensional glory.

"O'Brien! Why are you staring out of the window? Stop day-dreaming and concentrate!" So the trick was to lock eyes on the teacher and day-dream at the same time.

"O'Brien, what have I just been talking about? ... Can't you remember anything? ... Is nothing absorbed in that head of yours?"

Precious little information was absorbed in those days

because no one explained the absorption process. Buy a washing machine and the instructions come with it. Purchase a computer and you get a user's guide of encyclopaedic proportions. Your brain is vastly superior to any computer and incredibly complicated. So when we are born, where's the instruction manual? Much like using a computer, how could I be expected to output information if I wasn't told how to input it in the first place?

It is now my firm belief that what every student really needs to know before tackling any subject is how to learn how to learn. This book aims to reveal that process, so treat this as your own user's guide to the brain.

2 Speed Reading

"The art of reading is to skip judiciously."
— P. G. Hamerton (1834–94)

WHAT HOLDS UP OUR READING SPEED?
We know that the human eye can switch focus in less than 1/500 of a second. The width of text that each eye, at a normal reading distance of 45 centimetres (18 inches), can focus upon is approximately eighteen letters in an average typeface, such as the one in which this book is set. That's about three words, on average. In theory, therefore, the human eye should be capable of reading 1,500 words per second or 90,000 words per minute; yet the average reading speed is about 200 words per minute.

So what on earth happened to the other 89,800 words per minute?

Perhaps they got lost when we were taught to read – aloud – with our tongues instead of our eyes and brains.

The average reading speed, as I have said, lies somewhere between 200 and 250 words per minute, with a comprehension rate (understanding of the text) of between 50 and 70 per cent. Before we look at ways of how you can dramatically increase your reading speed, first test yourself to estimate your reading rate.

The following story – Seeing is Believing – contains 500 words. As you read it, time yourself carefully and note down the exact number of seconds you take. Then divide the number of words by the number of seconds you took, and multiply this by sixty: 500/sec $\times$ 60 = words/min.

If, for example, it took you 136 seconds, then your reading rate is 220 words per minute. Don't try to rush through the text, because there are questions at the end that test your comprehension of it.

Seeing is Believing

As we have seen, the potential reading speed of the human eye is, theoretically at least, 90,000 words per minute. Fantastic? Incredible? Impossible? Not so, apparently, for whiz-kid Eugenia Alexeyenko of Russia.

If the following account is true, I could have a serious rival at the next World Memory Championships! It is reported that eighteen-year-old Eugenia reads so fast that she could breeze through a massive 1,200-page novel like *War and Peace* by Leo Tolstoy or the equally bulky

A Suitable Boy by Vikram Seth in about ten minutes.

"This amazing girl can read infinitely faster than her fingers can flick the pages – and if she didn't have to slow herself down by doing this, she would read at the rate of 416,250 words a minute," said a senior researcher at the Moscow Academy of Science.

A special test was arranged for the superkid at the Kiev Brain Development Centre in front of a panel of scientists. They were sure that Eugenia had never read the test material before because they had obtained copies of political and literary magazines that appeared on the news-stands that day, after isolating her in a room at the testing centre. Researchers also brought in obscure and ancient books, as well as recently published ones, from Germany. These had been translated into Russian – the only language she knows.

While their subject was kept isolated, the examiners read the test material several times and took notes on its contents. They then placed two pages of the material in front of her to calculate her reading speed.

The result was astounding. She apparently read 1,390 words in a fifth of a second – the time it takes to blink one's eyes. She was also given several magazines, novels and reviews, which she read effortlessly.

What I find incredible was her evident comprehension of the contents. "We quizzed her in detail and often it was very technical information that most teenagers would never have been able to understand. Yet her answers proved that she understood perfectly," said one of the examiners.

Surprisingly, no one knew about Eugenia's unique ability until she was fifteen, when her father, Nikolai Alexeyenko, gave her a copy of a long newspaper article. When she handed it back to him two seconds later, saying it was quite interesting, he thought she was joking. However, when questioned, she gave all the right answers.

If this account is true, does it follow that she possesses phenomenal powers of eidetic or photographic memory? Not necessarily, according to Eugenia's own account of her extraordinary powers: "I don't know what my secret is. The pages go into my mind and I recall the sense rather than the exact text. There's some sort of analysis going on in my brain which I really can't explain. But I feel as though I have a whole library in my head!"

What do you think? Do you believe in Eugenia's inexplicable powers, or is this account the stuff of fiction?

Make a note of the time it took you to read the story, then answer these questions by ticking one of the alternatives:

1   What is Eugenia's surname?

☐ Zverevsky   ☐ Alexeyenko

2   How old is she?

☐ 16   ☐ 18

3   According to the senior researcher, how many words can she read per minute?

☐ 41,625   ☐ 416,250

4   Where was she tested?

☐ Moscow   ☐ Kiev

5   From which language was some of the test material
    translated?

☐ German   ☐ Dutch

6   How many languages, apart from Russian, can Eugenia
    speak?

☐ None   ☐ Nine

7   What is her father's name?

☐ Mikanov   ☐ Nikolai

8   At what age was her ability discovered?

☐ 15   ☐ 11

9   Where was the article that her father handed her from?

☐ A magazine   ☐ A newspaper

10 What does she say that she is able to recall as the pages
    go into her mind?

☐ The sense   ☐ The exact text

Now calculate your reading speed and check your answers against the text to work out your comprehension rating.

Words/min	Correct answers	Rating
0–150	1–4	Poor
150–250	5–7	Average
250–400	6–8	Better than average
400–750	7–10	Good
750–1000	8–10	Excellent
1000 or more	8–10	Genius

A quiet word in your ear

It now appears that some of the more traditional methods of teaching may in fact be a hindrance rather than a help to a pupil who is just starting to learn how to read.

One of the factors that may prevent us from speeding up our reading is that right from the start, we get into the habit of speaking every word we read. The phonetic and "look–say" methods are useful to us to begin with because we are learning two skills at the same time: speaking as well as reading. But why should we feel the need to say a word like "television" silently to ourselves on seeing it written down, when we're already perfectly capable of uttering the word out loud?

Try reading this sentence now without speaking the words to yourself or hearing any internal sounds. It may seem an impossible task at first, as the two operations have been inextricably linked from an early age; but with a little

SPEED READI

effort it is possible at least to turn the volume down. Do
let your reading rate be governed and kept to a finite spe
by an internal voice. You should be able to read even faster
than you actually speak. Former U.S. President John F.
Kennedy posthumously holds the talking speed record for a
public figure, but even he only managed 300 words per
minute. With technique and practice, it's quite reasonable
to expect to more than double this rate for reading.

I'm only going to tell you this once

When I'm giving a talk on memory, as part of my demonstration I ask the audience to call out random words one at
a time. While I'm memorising them a volunteer records the
order of the words until a total of 100 is reached. If all goes
well, I am then able to recall the exact sequence backwards
or forwards. But I'm faced with an acute balancing act here.
As I only hear each word once, I have to make quite sure
that the image I form is strong enough to recall later. This
involves time. In theory, the more time I take, the clearer
the image, but I've noticed that too much of a time lapse
between words can throw my concentration. So speeding
up into a steady rhythm or flow of words makes them easier
to remember. And because I know I'm only going to hear
each word once, it forces me to focus my mind.

Reading can be approached in the same way. First, it
doesn't follow that the longer you take digesting each word
the greater your comprehension of the text as a whole.
Speeding up can actually help you to develop a rhythm,

19

which will aid your concentration and, in turn, increase your understanding. Second, avoid back-tracking by telling yourself that you're only going to read a sentence once in order to absorb its contents. If you approach reading with the attitude of, "Well, I'll probably have to go over it again", then you're telling your mind that it doesn't have to focus so hard the first time because it's always got a second or third chance. If you miss the meaning of a phrase or sentence occasionally, keep moving. It's not worth losing your rhythm for the sake of the odd word – maintain a steady eye movement and your comprehension will improve.

Pointing the finger

I can remember, as a pupil at primary school, being told by my teacher that it was very bad practice to run my finger along the page as I was reading. I was told that although it might feel more comfortable reading this way, it would nevertheless inhibit my progress in the long term. And anyway, had I ever seen grown-ups use their fingers to read with? I suppose the logic behind the thinking was: How could a cumbersome lump of flesh and bone in the form of a finger ever hope to keep pace with the speed and agility of the eye and brain? Or perhaps it just looked awkward. Either way, the advice I was given was ill-informed.

Just think about your eye movement as you are reading this. Although you may think that your eyes are moving in a smooth, steady way, they are (as you will notice if you study someone else's eyes while they read) continually stopping and starting in a jerky fashion. The point at which your eyes stop or pause is the point at which the information is absorbed by the brain. So your reading speed is determined by the number of stops you take to cover a sentence and the amount of time spent on each of those stops.

It follows, then, that the advanced readers are those able to take in a much wider span of words during each interval. All this stopping and starting can put considerable strain on the eyes, so it's no wonder that reading is an effective method for getting off to sleep. One way of easing this workload on your eye muscles is to use a guide.

Guiding the eye

While keeping your head stationary, try to scan the room in front of you by slowly gliding your eyes from left to right without stopping at any point. You will find the task virtually impossible because your eyes will automatically want to stop and focus on the various objects along their path of vision. Repeat the exercise, but this time use a pointed finger held out in front of you to act as a guide. If you focus on the tip of your finger as you move it slowly from left to right, you'll notice that your eyes are now able to slide smoothly in one long sweep. Not only will your eyes feel more relaxed but you'll still be able to pick up all the objects in the background, albeit slightly out of focus.

Now apply the same principle to reading. Rest your finger on the page just below a line and start moving it from left to right until your eyes are able to follow the text without pausing. Gradually build up speed without worrying too much about the interpretation of the material, until the words become a blur. Interestingly, the point at which you can't distinguish any words is well in excess of 1,000 words per minute – so there are really no physical obstructions to hamper your progress. It's just your comprehension that needs to catch up.

Once you have found the upper limit, slow down to a rate which you find comfortable and the chances are that you've already gained over 50 per cent on your previous speed. Experiment with different types of pointers. I find a long thin biro or pencil with a fine tip the most effective eye guide. Develop a constant rhythm in your hand movement. Your brain will quickly accept that this new uninterrupted method of taking in information means that there is no time for stopping or back-tracking.

Imagine driving your car through a beauty spot. If you want to take in as much of the scenery around you as possible, one way is to take regular short glimpses, which means you've got to drive slowly for safety's sake. The other way is to stop every few miles and get out of the car to enjoy the view. The trouble is that this is just as slow and you miss out on all the sights between stops. The best way is to get someone else to do the driving for you – by being a passenger on a coach, for example. Although you forfeit control and may not be able to stop whenever you want, at least you can enjoy an uninterrupted flow of vistas and you reach your destination much faster, as well as having the physical strain of driving removed. So treat your hand as a personal chauffeur. Let it control the speed as you just sit back and enjoy the steady flow of information that passes before you.

It's actually possible to read two or three lines at the same time. The idea is that as you are reading the first line, you are prepared for the second line by getting a sneak preview of the words.

Over the coming days and weeks, persevere with your new reading method and monitor your progress at regular stages. Find the most efficient pointer, and if you have access to a metronome, use it during practice sessions to maintain a steady rhythm. See how fast you can read. By pushing your reading rate up to dizzy heights during practice, you will find that when you drop back to a more comfortable pace, what you thought was your normal reading speed will in fact have gone up a few notches.

Who knows, you may even be a potential world speed reading champion yourself!

3 Note-taking and Mind-mapping

*"A picture has been said to be something
between a thing and a thought."*

— Samuel Palmer (1805–81)

TAKE NOTE!

Whether attending lectures, revising for exams, preparing presentations or planning essays, notes have a vital role to play. But could we be more efficient with our note-taking? Could we use methods which make our notes more usable, easier to comprehend, more visual – something to help our brains picture all the relevant information in its entirety? The answer is yes.

What are notes for?

But first, the basics. There are extremely good reasons why notes are essential:

1 Notes act effectively as a filter, helping you to concentrate and prioritise key areas of importance while disregarding irrelevant padding.
2 They provide a quick reference for exam revision.
3 Because they are your own unique interpretation of information, they are in themselves memorable.
4 They aid understanding.
5 They facilitate an overview of a topic and appeal to both your imagination and your sense of logic and order.

The attention threshold

Have you ever sat through an entire lesson or lecture and remembered virtually nothing of what you heard? Silly question, really; but why does this happen? It was probably owing to one or more of these reasons:

1 The lecture was delivered in a listless monotone.
2 You had a total lack of interest in the subject.
3 The lecturer was a turn-off.
4 The lecturer was a turn-on.
5 You were suffering from a lack of sleep.
6 The subject matter was too complicated to absorb, or there was too much information.
7 Stress – either from the pressure of study or owing to social or domestic reasons. Stress is a major contributing factor to memory and recall loss – and if the root of your stress lies in achievement-related issues, like exams, fear of failure or parental pressure, it can be self-perpetuating.

Efficiency

Whatever the reason for your lack of concentration, efficient note-taking can ease the problem. As D-day – otherwise known as exams – looms ever closer, panicky note-taking creeps in, taking varied forms.

- *The great scoop*

Take the student who, journalist-style, has a compulsive desire to write down every precious word the lecturer has to offer lest he or she should miss out on a single pearl of wisdom. The result is a congealed soup of shorthand: it is impossible to fathom, the central theme is lost and time has been wasted gathering unnecessary information.

- *Danger! Faulty signalling*

Then there's the frenetic artist, the sort who indulges in the creation of a frenzied maze of arrows, boxes and more arrows that point to everything and nothing. Not the sort of person you want manning air traffic control as you're coming in to land. The intention is to connect individual pieces of data, facts, theories or ideas, thus creating a grand, unified overview. A valiant, logical aim and one that we shall find the route to shortly; but without basic guidelines the central point gets buried in a spaghetti-like disarray.

- *Precision engineering*

Similarly, there's the conscientious draughtsman. He or she also incorporates arrows and boxes but in a more precise

27

manner, taking great pains to make sure that all sides are of equal length and that angles contained in diamond or triangular shapes are also equal. Relevant associations and important data may, however, be overlooked for the sake of geometric accuracy.

- *I won't forget ... honest I won't*

Perhaps you are one of a group who rarely takes notes during a lecture, relying instead on faith in your memory. You may think you know it all in the short term, but how good is your long-term memory? What references will you have to fall back on in the future if you don't make notes now?

So what's the big deal about ordinary, linear notes? They're not that bad, are they? We get by on them, and besides, they're accepted universally. That's the way it is and things will never change.

Well, things are changing, and for the better. At this point it might be helpful to have a look inside our skulls.

THE BUILDING BLOCKS OF THOUGHT

Humans have an amazing ability to process information. The key agents in this process are the brain's nerve cells, or neurons. It is tempting to compare these cells with the working parts of computers, but neurons are fundamentally unrivalled because they work on a unique blend of electricity and chemistry. Each neuron has a main tentacle called an axon, and a myriad of smaller tentacles called dendrites. The axon of one neuron sends messages, which are received by the dendrites of others. The point at which these messages are received and sent is known as the synaptic gap, a tiny space only billionths of an inch wide where electrochemical changes take place that give rise to the very essence of thought itself.

It is hard to begin to comprehend the scope of the brain's thinking potential when one considers that:

1 A single neuron can make a possible 1,027 connections.
2 The brain contains about ten thousand million neurons.

It suggests that human thought is fundamentally limitless.

TWO BRAINS IN ONE?

The largest part of your brain, the cerebrum, consists of two hemispheres: the left and the right. Each hemisphere is covered with intricately folded "grey matter", the cortex, which handles decisions, memory, speech and other complex processes. The left hemisphere controls the right side of your body; the right hemisphere, your left side. These two hemispheres are joined together by a central connecting band of nerve fibres, the corpus callosum.

An American psychologist, Roger Sperry of the California Institute of Technology, carried out work during the 1960s with split-brain patients (people who have had their corpus callosum surgically severed, often as a treatment for epilepsy). Sperry discovered overwhelming evidence that each hemisphere has specialised functions.

29

In one experiment, patients were given an object to feel in one hand and then told to match it to a corresponding picture. Sperry noticed that:

1 The left hand helped the patient perform this task much better than the right hand.
2 The left and right hands gave rise to different strategies in solving the task.

However, when verbal descriptions of the objects were given to the patients, their right hands performed much better. The left hand (and therefore the right hemisphere of the brain) was more able to help the patient make the connection between the object it held and visual patterns.

Sperry's work was so ground-breaking that he won the Nobel Prize for Medicine in 1981 for his discoveries. Further work in this field has been done by a number of scientists, including Jerre Levy of the University of Chicago. A picture of the general information-processing functions of each hemisphere has now emerged.

Left hemisphere	Right hemisphere
Analytical	Visual
Logical	Imaginative
Sequential	Spatial
Linear	Perceptive
Speech	Rhythmic
Lists	Holistic (seeing an overview)
Number skills	Colour perception

Looking at this list of attributes, it is easy to see why many people have been tempted to label a person as being either left- or right-brained – that is, logical or creative. But this is an oversimplified and misleading interpretation. While it is fair to say that an accountant, for example, might draw heavily on the resources of the left brain and an artist those of the right, the two hemispheres certainly do not work in splendid isolation. If they did, our lives would be made wonderfully confused.

For example, if I were to say to you, "You can't be serious", and you were to use only the left hemisphere of your brain, you might assume that from now on I expected you to be amusing. However, by incorporating a bit of right-brain perception, you would realise that I was simply expressing my surprise.

The greatest thinkers in history – the Darwins and Einsteins – were the ones that took full advantage of both sides of their brains.

What can we expect from both hemispheres working in perfect harmony?

1 Visual analysis
2 Imaginative speech
3 Spatial logic
4 Colourful writing

We've looked at some of the more inefficient methods of taking notes. Now let's investigate one that utilises more of the brain's skills.

MIND MAPS

One man who has spent almost a lifetime on this subject is my friend and colleague Tony Buzan. Tony, who has written several bestsellers on the brain and learning processes, is the inventor of a revolutionary system of note-taking which he calls Mind Mapping®™.

Perhaps I am undervaluing his work by calling it a system of note-taking. It is more a method of learning, with many beneficial features.

The following is a description of a Mind Map:

1   The subject matter manifests itself in the form of a central image.
2   Main themes then radiate from this image in the form of branches.
3   Each branch is made unique by its own distinct label, colour and shape.
4   Each branch may radiate further sub-branches identified by a key image and/or word.
5   Branches or sub-branches may interconnect, depending on the strength of associations between them.

I have just listed five major characteristics of a Mind Map. I have tried to keep my descriptions as accurate and as succinct as possible, and I believe I've made a pretty good job of it. But I am limited by the very nature of my linear presentation of these descriptions. By putting the characteristics into words, not only does my account begin to sound rather technical, but I'm also asking you to draw on your reserves of imagination. Too much talk of "branches", "sub-branches" and "interconnecting", and I run the risk of switching you off completely.

Wouldn't everything be so much simpler if we could present the facts and express all our ideas in one hit, at a glance? Which is more accurate: a photograph, or a thousand-word description of a person's face?

A picture says it all – and so does a Mind Map. Take a look at the example of one on the following page. If you haven't seen a Mind Map before, you might be tempted to think that the picture is just an elaborate doodle; but this particular doodle happens to represent the life of Swiss artist Angelica Kauffmann (who is discussed in chapter nineteen). Now that you have actually seen a Mind Map, let's run through those descriptions again.

1 The subject matter – the artist – is the central image of the map.
2 Main themes – SUCCESSES, PAINTING, TRAVEL, LIFE – radiate from the central image like branches.
3 Each branch is a unique shape and is labelled.
4 Each branch sprouts further sub-branches – for example, "portrait", "anatomy", "mythology" and "neoclassical" sprout from PAINTING. Some of the sub-branches are embellished with key images.
5 There is scope for interconnecting the sub-branches – for example, those sprouting from TRAVEL and SUCCESSES relating to Italy and Italian cities.

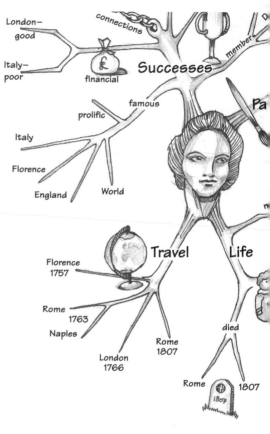

What are the benefits of a Mind Map?

1 The central core of the topic and its main themes are clearly defined.
2 The relative importance of each element is immediately apparent.
3 It enables rapid appraisal by giving an instant overview.
4 Unnecessary gobbledegook is eliminated.
5 It is unique, distinctive – and memorable.

What are its advantages over linear notes?

The advantages of the Mind Map are endless, probably because it satisfies everything the brain craves. It employs the full range of cortical skills, including the imaginative, spatial, verbal, logical, and so on.

It allows an unleashing of creativity. With linear notes you are committed to one idea at a time. Once you start a sentence, you're stuck with it until you get to the end. But our minds don't work that way; they are multidimensional. A Mind Map allows your thoughts to radiate out, freed from the bounds of one-way, single-level thought. It enables a steady stream of random ideas to flow unhindered, secure in the knowledge that the Mind Map will do all the structuring for you, like your very own personal organiser providing a model of your thoughts.

One-track mind

Stare at a page of text or linear notes and you get no gist, no initial sense of its meaning. So you have to read through it.

35

Even then, key words, central themes and important associations can be obscured, lost in the crowd of grammar, semantics, punctuation and other language features.

You could use the comparison of a great rail journey. You wish to explore new territory and you have decided to travel by train. The new territory is the new subject you wish to learn, and the railway line represents linear notes on the subject. The destination is your understanding of the subject, and the various stops or stations along the way are the key words or themes. Each sleeper that makes up the track symbolises each word of your notes.

You decide that in order to appreciate this new land and get a feel for the culture, you should stop off at as many stations as possible and explore the towns and villages. The trouble is that you spend most of your time travelling, just sitting on the train, moving in a straight line, and it seems to take for ever to get from one station to the next. In other words you're spending time on the irrelevant words that make up the track, rather than focusing on the themes that will gain you marks in exams.

You wish you had a better overall picture. You've got no idea where you are – you didn't bring a map! When you do finally reach your journey's end, you feel as though you've missed out. How can you get a proper feel for a country if all you do is travel in one straight line? Wouldn't it be better to charter a helicopter and take a map? It's quicker, you get a great overview and you can land wherever you want to look at important places in detail.

Guidelines for mind-mapping

Instead of taking a mind-numbing railway journey through your subject, use a helicopter and a map. By following a few simple guidelines, you'll be able to create Mind Maps that will enable you to fully understand your subject by charting the key words, the main themes and, most importantly of all, the relationships between themes.

- *Always start with a central image.*

This is the focal point of attention. Choose a piece of paper that is large enough to allow all the themes to radiate from the centre.

- *Use only one key word per line.*

It's tempting to write more than one word because that's what we're used to. Don't. It's good discipline to get straight to the point.

- *Use symbolic images as often as possible.*

It's easy. You don't have to be Michelangelo. Even very simple images not only create visual impact but are highly effective memory aids.

- *Use different colours for different themes.*

The majority of standard notes are written out in a single colour, usually black or blue – monotonous, dull and forgettable. Colours accentuate and highlight. They are memorable, adding character, appeal and ... colour!

37

- *Use creative imagination and association.*

The beauty of a Mind Map is that it can accommodate even the wildest imagination. In fact, the more untamed you allow your imagination to be, the better. Brainstormed ideas bursting to get out don't have to queue up in a polite, orderly fashion. They can be released immediately while they're still hot. Just form a branch and wrap the idea around it. Keep going, branch out if necessary and, if an associated thought leaps out in front of you, throw a rope across to another branch instead of casting the thought aside for later attention.

Don't let ideas get channelled; you'll only thwart the natural flow of creativity. It's a bit like working in a sorting office. The ideas arrive by the sack-load in differently shaped packages, parcels and letters. There are so many that you wonder where they all came from. Luckily, the sorting office is fully automated, and all you have to do is empty them onto the conveyor belt.

So open the floodgates and empty your thoughts onto the fully automated, self-organising Mind Map. There's no need to worry about filling it up. It has no saturation point, just as our thought potential is limitless. Infinite thought – and infinite space in which to map our thoughts.

WHEN TO USE A MIND MAP
Mind maps are extremely versatile. Don't just use them for revision – use them all the time!

Receiving oral information

Whether you are attending a lecture or a group discussion, the Mind Map provides an excellent method for recording data and structuring topics. It reduces a talk to the salient facts and highlights the relationships between those facts. The results can be both revealing and surprising.

They may even expose the more tangential side of your teacher. For example, he or she may announce that the entire lecture is to be devoted to the functions of blood cells. But instead of ending up with a nice, even distribution of branches covering the three main components of blood cells – red cells, white cells and platelets – it becomes apparent that 70 per cent of your Mind Map relates to sickle-cell anaemia, a subject of great interest to your teacher but one irrelevant to your studies.

I doubt that you'll gain any Brownie points by exhibiting your findings, but you may nudge your teacher into sticking to the syllabus!

Receiving visual information

Information presented to us visually, in the form of practical demonstrations, videos, films, slide presentations, and so on, have a greater impact on us because they offer wider cortical appeal – movement, colour, and a spatial as well as aural element. We remember things more easily if we attach images to them. The sight of litmus paper turning red in an acid is retained far longer in the memory than a written or oral account of that reaction.

The Mind Map in this case acts as a diary, sparking off images from past scientific experiments or reminding us of scenes from historical re-enactments. Key symbolic images – however badly drawn – play an important role here in triggering off these visual recollections.

Processing written information

The advantage of learning from textbooks, novels, plays, journals, and the like is that we can work at our own pace. We have ultimate control over how much, how little and which material to read.

The disadvantage is that we lose the impact of someone else's presentation – animation, verbal emphasis, visual stimulation and interaction. This, then, makes the learning process a bit more of an effort because we are left, literally, to our own mental devices. It is our imagination that we turn to and rely on to act as a substitute for movement, emphasis and stimulation if we are to maintain some semblance of impact. Not easy, I grant you, if the text you are clutching happens to be on quantum mechanics.

But before engaging the imagination, valuable time can be saved by working in the following way:

1 Plan your reading. Check the contents section for chapters relevant to your studies. You could also quickly scan the index and make a note of certain page numbers. Concentrate on these. Don't feel duty bound to read the book word for word, cover to cover. Paying attention to

unnecessary detail usually signals a fear of missing something. The danger is that this preoccupation may result in your missing the very thing you're looking for – the central point.

2 Look out for the central message, and when you think you've located it you have a starting point for your Mind Map. Read on with an open, enquiring mind and try to bring the text alive by using your creative imagination.

3 Try not to read passively. Think things through and question the logic behind various statements. If you play an active role during reading, this will greatly enhance your understanding and memory of a subject because you will be allowing your mind to make connections and associations. For association is the mechanism by which memory works.

4 Keep adding to your Mind Map, jotting down key words and ideas as you unravel more supporting topics. Important data such as names, terms, dates and formulae can all be accommodated, written on lines extending from branches. Make sure they can be recognised at a glance. Branches may also be numbered, should you wish to show order and priority.

After a reading session, the Mind Map may reveal that what you thought was the central message is in fact an offshoot of a main branch, or vice versa. In such a case you will need to form another Mind Map, this time built round the true core of the subject.

Preparing essays

It follows that if an essay consists of an introduction, main text and conclusion, then this should be the order in which we should write it. But how can you write an introduction to something you haven't yet written about?

It's a bit like announcing a list of New Year's resolutions. They all sound promising, but come the New Year your ideas may change and you'll wish you'd kept your mouth shut. So rather than make promises you may not want to keep, plan the main body of your essay first – that way you'll guarantee an accurate introduction.

Drawing up a plan really is the only way to start writing an essay. It's easier for you and it makes for a better read. Picturing the structure of your essay will allow you to keep a balanced spread of topics and make a smooth transition from point to point.

Blindly trudging off down the path of the first thing that enters your head can lead to imbalance, repetition and a disjointed account. Time will be wasted making alterations halfway through, as you realise that the running order is wrong and the relationship between points has only just dawned on you. And don't forget, examiners award no marks for repetition – by repeating yourself you're simply wasting time and words you could be using to make a clear point or to explain how you see your ideas fitting together.

If you're going to make mistakes, sort them out at the planning stage; don't wait until you've nearly finished to see the daylight. Planning an essay may seem difficult because:

1 You fear you don't know enough about the subject to know how to begin.

2 You've got so many ideas that you don't know where to begin.

This is where the Mind Map comes into its own. We always underestimate the true extent of our knowledge. A Mind Map has the effect of squeezing out knowledge, "like an independent little miner ferreting away in the mines of your mind and digging out information that otherwise would have been sealed in for ever" as Tony Buzan puts it. It dramatically counters your suspicions of ignorance by disclosing a lot more than you thought you knew, thus giving you the confidence to write – you do have something to say.

On the other hand, being spoilt for choice by having so much to say may camouflage the structure of the essay. To avoid this "wood for the trees" syndrome, use the Map to give you an overview of all your thoughts. Again, starting with a central image, chuck down all the ideas as they present themselves to you. Don't worry about priority at this stage: just empty your mind and watch the themes radiate from the centre like shock waves. By releasing what is uppermost in your mind, you are collecting the bones of the body of your work. Once you can see all these bones laid out in front of you, the job of assembling and connecting them is that much easier.

The process of essay-writing can be viewed as an assembly line. The Mind Map is the skeletal stage; putting on the grammatical flesh and adding cosmetic semantics is the last linear stage, the point at which you physically write it.

Preparing presentations

In chapter nineteen, I explain in detail how you can deliver a speech or give a presentation entirely from memory. First, however, you've got to make sure that your presentation is worth remembering!

Preparing for a presentation is much like preparing an essay, but with a slight variation. Formulate the structure using a Mind Map in the way described for planning an essay. This time, however, depending on the time you have available for the presentation, you may need to confine your speech to just three, or possibly four, key features. Think of your audience and put yourself in their shoes: it's better to make sure that the message gets across by concentrating on a couple of themes rather than trying to cover too many topics with no time for adequate explanation.

You may have to draw two Maps. The first one will provide you with, hopefully, a glut of possible choices, and more importantly will indicate, by the sheer density of certain branches, the biggest "talking points".

The second Map will need to be a tighter, more edited version of the first, leaving you with a clear structure containing the themes you feel most comfortable talking about.

Once you are happy with your plan, the Mind Map itself can be used to guide you through the presentation. It is an extremely effective memory aid, obviating the need to shuffle notes scrawled on numerous bits of paper. In presentations, as in other parts of your academic life, Mind Maps will become a reliable and flexible tool for success – you'll wonder how you ever got by without them.

4　Memory

"Memory is the mother of all wisdom."
— Aeschylus (525–456BCE)

ORDINARY OR EXTRAORDINARY?

Before 1987 I believed that people who performed prodigious feats of memory must have been born with a special "gift". I thought that their brains were, in some way, wired up very differently from the rest of us. They were, in my view, the select few who, by some freak of nature, were lucky enough to be bestowed with this extra facility not available to just anyone.

As long ago as May 1974, Bhanddanta Vicittabi Vumsa of Rangoon, Burma, set an impressive memory record by reciting 16,000 pages of Buddhist canonical texts. A similarly unbelievable record was set by twenty-six-year-old

Gon Yangling of China, who memorised more than 15,000 telephone numbers. Having spent years studying memory development, I am no longer bewildered and confused when hearing reports like this because I now understand how it is possible to train the memory to perform such great feats. Rather than assuming that there must be a physiological difference in these people (the only exceptions are the rare cases of people with a photographic memory), I now believe that what separates the average memory from one capable of storing the data held within a telephone directory can be summed up in three simple words: desire and technique.

DESIRE AND TECHNIQUE

It surely follows, as for most things in life, that the degree to which a person excels in whatever they do is directly proportional to their degree of desire. The finest sportsmen and sportswomen all share one thing in common – a burning will to succeed, driven by an unyielding passion for their particular sport. If the need, want, determination and love are great enough, then acquiring and applying the necessary technique becomes a joy, not a task.

The same holds true for studying. While you may find the thought of having a love affair with physics out of the question, by at least getting interested in particular aspects of the subject you can definitely make the process of learning more enjoyable. But how do we create this desire for something? Where does it come from?

48

Enthusiasm for a sport is usually motivated by inspiration. The dream of becoming a world-class footballer may stem from the sight of Wayne Rooney stylishly thundering a ball into the net. An addiction to tennis might be triggered by a single, memorable backhand passing shot unleashed by Venus Williams.

Whether it prompts inspiration, fascination, curiosity or emulation, somewhere along the line an initial impression is made that stays permanently with us, spurring us on and driving our will to succeed.

In my case, the long chain of cause and effect culminating in the writing of this book was instigated by the sight of Creighton Carvello memorising a pack of playing cards on television. The fascination was in seeing somebody achieve the seemingly impossible – the memorisation of fifty-two ostensibly unconnected bits of information in less than three minutes, using nothing more than the power of the mind. The curiosity came in trying to figure out how on earth he did it.

So there you have it. The inspiration had made its impact and I was hooked for life!

JOGGING THE BRAIN

On reflection, my initial ambitions now seem somewhat limited. All I was concerned with was beating Creighton's time and getting myself into the record books.

I hadn't realised that what I was about to embark on, over the coming weeks and months, was an object lesson in accelerated learning. I thought that at the end of my period of memory training, a tiny part of my brain would have acquired a new skill: that, and only that, of memorising packs of playing cards.

Nobody told me about the wider implications of training my memory:

1 Deeper concentration
2 Longer-term retention
3 Clearer thinking
4 Greater self-confidence
5 Wider observation

In short, I was unwittingly exercising my brain the way an athlete exercises his or her body. It's like deciding that because you can't fit comfortably into your clothes any more, it's time to lose weight. But after six weeks of regular daily exercise, it's not just your clothes that look and feel good on you; your body does too.

And what about all the other benefits, like better circulation, a healthier complexion, a guilt-free appetite, and generally feeling more active?

For the past couple of decades we have been concentrating solely on the body beautiful. Joining a gym and regularly working out seem to be increasing priorities in many people's lives. But why do we continue to settle for just a fit body when we can get our brains in shape as well?

Although the brain is an organ, it can be treated in much the same way as any muscle. The more you exercise it, the stronger it becomes. Conversely, the saying "Use it or lose it" is an apt warning for a lazy mind.

One of the most enjoyable ways of exercising the body is to take up a sport or group activity. The competitive angle diverts your attention away from the arduous, mundane side of exercise and focuses it on winning. Surely, then, this is an equally effective incentive for mental exercise?

Head-to-head games such as chess, bridge and Scrabble and group games involving problem-solving, lateral thinking or strategy are all excellent ways of challenging and stimulating thought processes. Chess is an especially fine mind sport, as it sharpens a wide range of cortical skills: logic in forward planning (if I do A, then B, C, D or E happens), sequence, memory and imaginative, spatial and overview skills. There's no excuse these days: if you can't find an opponent and don't have time to join a club, you can always buy a computer program or play online. This way you'll get a game whenever you want but, unless you're a Grand Master, it won't be a pushover.

If you enjoy group work and pooling ideas, why not set up or join a Use Your Head club? These clubs, to whom I occasionally lecture, are aimed at anyone who wishes to learn how to get the most out of their brains and have been emerging in increasing numbers at schools and universities.

The rise of the "mentathlete"

Memory itself has been growing rapidly as a mind sport ever since the first World Memory Championships took place at the Athenaeum, the famous London club, in 1991. Now held annually, this competition takes place in venues around the world. As the event grows in stature, so does the interest of the world's press and the amount of sponsorship it attracts. And with the increase in the value of the prizes, so too has the strength of the competition grown, as more memory stars, or "mentathletes", have begun filtering through from different parts of the globe, eager to make a name for themselves and snatch a memorable payday.

The Championships are the flagship event of the World Memory Sports Council, which currently has branches in eight countries, spanning the globe from China to Canada, the UK and the USA. If the power of the memory intrigues you – as it did me all those years ago and still does today – check out the World Memory Sports Council website (www.worldmemorychampionship.com). The UK branch of the Memory Sports Council, set up in 2005, regulates the mind sport of memory in the UK. So why not become a member and gain official recognition of your status as a mentathlete? The Council can also put you in touch with local and regional memory clubs.

And international mind sports don't stop there. The annual Mind Sports Olympiad – an Olympics for thinking games – offers another forum for the world's mentathletes. Competitors play each other at chess, backgammon, Scrabble and other strategy-based games, competing for gold, silver and bronze medals. The Mind Sports Olympiad website (www.msoworld.com) offers the opportunity to test your skills online and find out about local and regional mind sports clubs.

So memory has plenty going for it. It is an art form, a sport, a method of mental exercise and a cortical tuning fork, and if practised regularly will deliver the key to learning how to learn and, ultimately how to pass exams.

HOW GOOD IS YOUR MEMORY?

As a control test, spend no more than two minutes trying to memorise the following list of twenty items in order.

1 Diamond
2 Brain
3 Hairbrush
4 Fire
5 Horse
6 Window
7 Gondola
8 Baby
9 Treasure
10 Doctor
11 Cook
12 Desk
13 Faint
14 Carpet
15 Planet
16 Dragon
17 Book

18 Violin

19 Lawnmower

20 Shadow

Now, write down as many of the words as you can remember, in the same order that they appeared. Then compare your score with the following:

20	Perfect
16–19	Excellent
11–15	Very good
7–10	Good
3–6	Average
0–2	Try a softer drink

If you achieved only an average score, don't worry. By the end of this book you won't be far off making a perfect score. The reason we have difficulty in trying to memorise a list of random words is that there is no obvious connection between them. So we try to rely either on "brute force" memory or by repeating the words over and over again in the hope that there will be some verbal, rhythmical recollection – "Diamond … diamond, brain … diamond, brain, hairbrush" and so on. Unfortunately, as these words are neither rhythmical nor rhyming, using a verbal method of memory will always be an uphill struggle. The most effective method is one that uses imagination and association.

5 Imagination and Association

"It's not what you look at that matters, it's what you see."
— Henry David Thoreau (1817–62)

IMAGINATION – THE KEY

The Greek philosopher Aristotle believed that the human soul never thought without first creating a mental picture. All knowledge and information, he argued, entered the soul – that is, the brain – via the five senses: touch, taste, smell, sight and sound. The imagination would come into play first, decoding the messages delivered by our senses and turning the information into images. Only then could the intellect get to work on the information.

In other words, in order to make sense of everything around us, we are continually creating models of the world inside our heads.

Most of us start to make mental models from an early age, and soon become highly adept at it. We can recognise an individual solely by the characteristic sounds their footsteps make. We can make an intuitive judgment of a person's mood from the briefest of movements. But what you are doing right now is an even more spectacular example. With considerable ease, your eyes are scanning an enormous sequence of jumbled letters, and your brain is recognising groups of words and simultaneously forming images as fast as you can physically read them.

Perhaps the most spectacular display of what our imaginations can do lies, if we can remember them, in our dreams. There are various gadgets available that can help us enjoy and experience our dreams. Volunteers have tested one such device, which consists of goggles containing sensors that pick up rapid eye movements (REMs). REM sleep is the period when our dreams seem to be at their most active, occurring only at certain times, and then only for short bursts. Once REMs are detected, the sensors trigger off tiny flashing lights fitted into the goggles. The intention is to make the volunteer gradually aware that he or she is in a dream state without waking them up. This semiconscious awareness allows for a fascinating ringside view of the virtual reality world of the imagination, with reports of "seeing everything in full-blown technicolor and immaculate detail". Faces of friends or relatives that haven't been seen for years are faithfully reproduced with incredible accuracy, and all the senses are experienced as uncannily real.

I used the example of dreaming merely to counter the poor excuses that some people give me, such as "I could never adopt your methods, I just don't have the imagination for it". Wrong. We all possess a highly inventive imagination, as exhibited in our dreams, although sadly, for some people, this is the only time it's let out to play.

The debate over whether you can teach creativity or not is a false one. We have all proved just how naturally creative we were as children, living in our own colourful imaginary worlds. The question should be: how can we encourage the return of creativity into our adult lives?

Perhaps being told too early in our lives to "grow up" or "start acting like an adult" is partly to blame, by leaving us with the notion that an active imagination is a sign of childishness and that the ones who don't grow out of it end up in uncertain careers as comedians, entertainers or artists. I believe that it's not a question of what you should do to become creative, but what you should undo. To become an "un" person you need to be:

Unlocked	Unbound	Unrestrained
Unleashed	Unprejudiced	Unchained
Unrestricted	Unpredictable	Unplugged
Untamed	Unobstructed	Uncensored
Unbarred	Unusual	Uncorked
Unhindered	Unimpeded	Uninhibited

Interestingly, removing the "un" prefix from many of these words gives you a description of what inevitably happens to creative freedom in countries that are governed by oppressive regimes – that is, censored, restrained, bound, barred, restricted, obstructed, tamed.

So if creative thought is to blossom, we first need to remove the blinkers and tear down the boundaries we may inadvertently have set up for ourselves in order to allow our ideas to flow freely and unchecked. Once liberated, our thoughts can then be allowed to meander, explore and wander in any direction at all – preferably taking the most scenic route.

The following exercise is a useful test of the imagination, and will also put you in the right frame of mind for absorbing memory techniques in the next few chapters. If you are familiar with brainstorming and creative thinking exercises, then you should find this easy. Just let your imagination have free rein.

Assuming you now own the original of Leonardo da Vinci's *Mona Lisa*, write down as many possible uses for it as you can think of. Give yourself no more than two minutes. Then score as follows:

20 or more	Highly creative
16–19	Excellent
11–15	Very good
7–10	Good
3–6	Average
0–2	Couch potato

The most common answer is:

> *"for selling and making millions"*

The socially responsible person:

> *"for donating to a museum"*

The unadventurous type:

> *"for hanging on the sitting-room wall"*

The unleashed, unhindered:

> *"for lagging pipes in severe winter"*

The secret to scoring well in an exercise like this lies in letting your imagination literally run riot, rather than wasting time trying to contrive and plan an idea based on practicality, logic or ethics. Follow your mind's eye and simply record whatever you see. After a while you'll have a job to keep up with the torrent of ideas that flow out, unrestrained and untamed.

When I memorised the order of a pack of cards in 38 seconds – a world record – there was no time to plan anything. I acted like a photographer hurriedly trying to take snapshots of fifty-two marathon runners. With only forty-three seconds to play with, there's no time to set up carefully designed portrait shots: you just click what you see.

Similarly, for imagination to flower you need to relinquish a bit of control and just watch. Being told to use one's imagination implies some kind of effort is needed. But we are continuously and automatically manufacturing ideas. The difficulty comes in trying to see them. So any effort should be directed toward training the visual side of our imagination. I would say that about 95 per cent of the time spent on training my memory is concentrated on this very aspect: visualisation.

ASSOCIATION

We define an object not by what it is but by what we associate it with. When I see a smoking pipe I don't immediately think to myself, "This is a tube with a bowl at one end for the smoking of a fill of tobacco"; I think of Sherlock Holmes, a small tobacconist's shop I know, the smell of Balkan Sobranies or the famous painting of a pipe by René Magritte entitled *Ceci n'est pas une pipe* (*This is Not a Pipe*).

When I see a pair of wellingtons, I don't automatically think, "These are rubber boots loosely covering the calves and protecting against the intrusion of water"; I think of a muddy footpath, a fishing trip, horse-racing, woodland walks – anything but the dictionary definition. And when I see an oyster, it's not a bivalve shellfish to me – it's why my mouth is watering.

I perceive something – a telephone or a cat – not by its function or chemical constituents, but by the sum total of all my previous associations with it. The more I encounter and experience something, the more mental hooks I attach to it. I have gathered such a wealth of these mental hooks over the years that they now form an aura surrounding the object, almost giving it a character of its own. What do you associate, for example, with a telephone? Contact with the outside world, exciting news, sad news, paying the bill? If you think long and hard enough you could probably write a book about it. What feelings are triggered at the sound of a telephone ringing? A sense of joy, panic, curiosity, relief or annoyance? Pondering on these associations provides us with an extremely neat link to the next chapter.

6   The Link Method

"'Objects in pictures should so be arranged as
by their very position to tell their own story."
— Johann Wolfgang von Goethe (1749–1832)

LET IT COME TO YOU

If you found it difficult to memorise the list of words in chapter four, it was because there was no obvious connection between the items. So the answer is to create an artificial one by allowing your imagination to get to work.

This is known as the link method. It is a simple way to memorise a list of items. This can be particularly useful in a subject like history, in which you may need to remember a long chain of events. Even if the subjects you are studying do not require you to absorb lists of material in order, the link method is nevertheless a useful memory exercise as it utilises your creative imagination and, in particular, your powers of association. And you need never worry that some unconnected words just can't be linked – you will see how easily strange and memorable images will just come to you.

Take a look at the chapter four list again, but this time link each word together by featuring them in a bizarre story. To start off, imagine using a large pointed **diamond** to dissect a **brain**. As you start to cut open the brain, you discover a multicoloured **hairbrush** buried deep within the cerebrum. As you remove the hairbrush you notice that some of the bristles have been singed, possibly by a **fire** … and so the story goes on.

Using the list below, take up the story using your own narrative. To help make your account memorable, exaggerate the scenes and try to bring into play all your senses – touch, taste, smell, see and hear everything. But above all, concentrate on visualising as much of the detail that your imagination throws at you. Take your time and, if (as I find) it helps, close your eyes after looking at each word as you try to form your mental pictures.

1 Diamond
2 Brain
3 Hairbrush
4 Fire
5 Horse
6 Window
7 Gondola
8 Baby

9   Treasure

10 Doctor

11 Cook

12 Desk

13 Faint

14 Carpet

15 Planet

16 Dragon

17 Book

18 Violin

19 Lawnmower

20 Shadow

Now compare your new score with your original effort. You will have fared much better this time. If you did miss out a word it was probably for one of the following reasons:

- *The image you created was too dull.*

Make your images stand out by exaggerating them and creating movement. Notice how colourful I made the hairbrush, and how large the diamond.

- *You thought you'd remember it anyway.*

This is a common error, particularly if you think a word like "dragon" is striking enough to remember on its own without creating some extra details. How can you expect your memory to recall something that you haven't bothered to register in the first place?

- *The image was too vague.*

You may have remembered the word "instrument" instead of the word "violin". It's important to see as much of the detail as possible. Note the shape of the violin and listen to the sound the strings make.

- *You couldn't visualise the word.*

Certain words are not easy to visualise, in which case you'll need to be inventive and apply a bit of ingenuity. If you can't come up with anything for the word "faint", for example, then imagine painting a big letter F. As the word "paint" rhymes with "faint", this substitute should then act as an appropriate trigger for the original word. Association is, after all, what binds memory.

- *There was no set backdrop.*

The difficulty with the link system is that it tends to dictate what sort of surrounding scenery there should be. When you were trying to visualise the gruesome act of dissecting a brain, whereabouts, in your mental geography, were you performing this surgery? Perhaps you had a vague impression of a laboratory or operating theatre in the background. Where was the gondola situated? Did you suddenly have to fly off to Venice? I find, as you probably do, that I'm so focused on the words in the list that I largely ignore any background detail that may arise in association, leaving the images floating in a sort of white, misty haze. The danger is

that they end up looking like cartoon drawings in a va
um. If your story has no set, unique background, how
you keep this list mentally separated from any further ones
you come to memorise?

Setting the background

For images to stay firmly lodged in the brain, they need to
make as realistic an impact on the memory as we can create. The secret is to provide a familiar mental background
in which to anchor these images. As an example, let's commit to memory the royal houses of Great Britain in the
order of their reigns.

1   Norman
2   Plantaganet
3   Lancaster
4   York
5   Tudor
6   Stuart
7   Hanover
8   Windsor

This may not be a list you ever thought you wanted to learn,
but it serves as a useful example because very few of us can
name these dynasties, let alone in order, so the information
is fresh. By combining the link method with an imaginative
story set in a very specific place, we can lift information
from its dull, two-dimensional state, breathe life into it and
make it more memorable.

This is how I remember the correct order. As you read through the following short story, keep an open mind and try to picture the scenes and events that unfold using your powerful imagination.

As it's royal dynasties or houses we are dealing with, I have chosen Buckingham Palace as a geographical setting to start the story. Picture **Norman** Bates (or Greg Norman, or any other Norman who is more familiar to you) leaving the Palace through the front gates. He has just had tea with the Queen. To remember Plantaganet, imagine Norman stepping onto a **plane** conveniently waiting for him outside the gates. The plane turns out to be a **Lancaster** bomber and, as Norman takes off over London, he decides to go on a bombing raid. But the bombs he starts releasing, instead of being conventional ones, are made of chocolate. They are **Yorkie** Bar bombs. One of the Yorkie Bars crashes into an old **Tudor**-style house, distinguished by characteristic half-timbering and large rectangular windows. A Scotsman called **Stuart** rushes out of the house, disturbed by all the commotion. He looks the worse for wear as he staggers around bleary-eyed and scratching his head. The empty bottle he's carrying in his hand signals that he is suffering from a severe **hangover**. He decides to shake off his bad head by **windsurf**ing in the fountains at Trafalgar Square!

The story in itself is ridiculous, bizarre and wholly unlikely, but that's why I can remember it, and even though it is my invention you will probably remember it too. It didn't take long to create, either. I simply pictured the first ideas and associations that entered my head as I read each name down the list. It's important to hold on to these first associations, as they are the ones most likely to repeat themselves at a later date.

Notice how the sequence of events running through the story has followed the sequence of the list, allowing me to recite the order backward or forward and at great speed. Which royal family follows York? By referring back to the scene over London, you'll know the answer is Tudor because you can see the Yorkie bombs dropping on the old Tudor house. Likewise you should be able to tell in an instant that Lancaster must therefore come before York. Now see if you can repeat the list backward by simply reversing the story.

In chapter nine I will show you how to memorise dates by introducing the language of numbers, but for now content yourself in the knowledge that by using a simple story, your memory of otherwise forgettable information can be dramatically improved.

7   Visualisation

"I have a grand memory for forgetting."
— Robert Louis Stevenson (1850–94)

YOUR PERFECT MEMORY

If you had to write down everything, and I mean every little detail, that you could remember about today – what you had for breakfast, conversations, confrontations, sights, sounds, thoughts, emotions – it would probably take you all day. The individual memories, if you thought for long enough about it, would literally run into the thousands.

There seems to be a great imbalance here. If, on the one hand, our memories are so perfect that we can recall tying a shoelace at 1.40 p.m. and removing a speck of dust from the marmalade on a piece of toast, why can't we remember that the atomic weight of hydrogen is 1.00797?

The simple answer to why you can remember so much information about today is because you were there. Your day has been filled with a rich tapestry of experiences, each of which was made truly memorable by a vast network of interwoven associations. You know it was 1.40 p.m. when you tied your shoelace because that's when you were watching *Jerry Springer* on TV instead of attending a lecture.

It's easy to recall the order of events throughout the day as well. All you have to do is think back to where you were and what you were doing. You're hardly going to ask yourself, "Now did I receive medical attention after I tripped over the poodle and split my head open, or was it a couple of hours before?" unless, of course you're accident-prone or suffering from severe concussion.

You remember travelling to college by train so vividly because you saw the passengers and fields outside, spoke to the ticket inspector, felt the vibrations and smelled the distinct aroma that only trains give off. And if that wasn't enough evidence for your memory, you set all your observations hard in concrete by adding your thoughts to them.

So how many senses do we have to block off before we can't remember what we have experienced? Spending a day at school blindfolded wouldn't be enough. Wearing earplugs as well would certainly prevent you from learning very much, but it still wouldn't stop you from recalling the whole day's experience. In fact, no matter how desensitised you became, your memory would still be left with the one thing that can't be blocked off – your imagination.

To prove this, here is a lateral thinking question for you. All the events in it actually took place.

I sat in a room all day with my eyes closed and my ears plugged. There were several witnesses present with me throughout the day. I imagined meeting 2,808 people in a set order. The only time I opened my eyes was when I was shown a character.

Question: What was I doing?

Answer: I was trying to memorise the order of fifty-four packs of playing cards that had all been shuffled together to form a random sequence of 2,808 cards.

With only a single sighting of each card allowed, they were dealt out one at a time, one on top of another. After twelve hours of memorising the cards, I was then ready to start reciting the sequence, which took a further three hours, including breaks.

This record attempt took place in London in May 2002. I managed to recite the correct sequence with just eight errors. This is how I did it:

1 Before the record attempt, I prepared fifty-four separate routes in my head.
2 Each route consisted of a particular journey made through a familiar mental location such as a town, park or golf course.

73

3 I made sure that each journey had fifty-two stops or places along the way.

4 Every playing card was represented in my mind by a person. The king of clubs became Saddam Hussein and the four of diamonds my bank manager.

5 To memorise the order of the cards, I simply had to imagine meeting them as people along each stage of each journey.

6 The order of the journeys naturally preserved the order in which the cards fell. If the first card of the first pack was the four of diamonds, then I imagined my bank manager standing in front of the first tee at Wentworth Golf Club, because that was the first stage of my first journey.

I can assure you that there is not the remotest chance of my being able to memorise the order of more than eight or nine cards unless I use a method like this one. Although 2,808 bits of information seems like an awful lot to remember, it is nothing compared to the amount of data that you could recall after a typical day's experiences.

What I had effectively done was to trick my memory into semi-believing that it had witnessed a series of experiences, and the depth of this belief was totally dependent on the ability of my imagination to conjure up artificially sensed experiences. I say semi-believe, because the day I start believing that I've played golf with Saddam Hussein is the day my friends and family start to worry!

THE BRAD PITT FACTOR

When I explain this method to students, some say that although they appreciate the theory behind it, they are nonetheless unwilling to experiment because they can't produce photographically realistic images of either scenery or people. This is an important point and it's crucial to stress that not only am I unable to create vivid mental images but that seeing is only part of the process of forming an overall mental "picture". It is not high-definition graphic detail that makes a strong impact on our memories so much as an impression built up by a mixture of senses.

For example, if I were to say to you, "Don't turn around, but Brad Pitt is standing right behind you," you might not be able to produce a faithfully accurate mental picture of him, but you would certainly feel his presence. It would produce so many mixed reactions that it would leave a lasting impression on your memory. What the hell's he doing in my bedroom?

This is the main reason why I use people to represent playing cards. When I first started experimenting with memory systems I chose various household objects such as a chair, book or table as symbols for remembering cards, but they all lacked that Brad Pitt factor. Not surprisingly, Brad Pitt is easier to remember than a kitchen table. People have their own distinct character; they are animate, versatile, react in certain ways to different surroundings, and you can interact with them in many more ways. A kitchen table, wherever it is, is still a kitchen table.

75

It is people, then, who hold the key to memorising information – any information, whether it be a random sequence of playing cards, a complicated speech from a Shakespeare play, chemical formulae, historical dates or whatever key facts you wish to have at your fingertips when you walk into that exam.

8   The Journey Method

"Any landscape is a condition of the spirit."
— Henri-Frédéric Amiel (1821–81)

THE SCENIC ROUTE TO A PERFECT MEMORY
The technique I briefly described in the previous chapter –
of imagining journeys through familiar landscapes and
locations in order to "fix" items and their order in the
memory – isn't exclusive to me by any means. You too can
use it, and in this chapter I show you how.

The following exercise is a test of imagination rather
than of memory. However, after looking through the list on
the following page you should be able to achieve total recall.
You will do this by using the journey method, or system of
loci, that the ancient Greeks knew and practised to improve
their memories more than 2,000 years ago.

loci

But first:

1 You will need to prepare a mental route consisting of twelve stages. The route could, for example, be a typical journey from home to school, college or a friend's house.

2 Choose significant or memorable landmarks as stages along the route, such as a church, bus stop or post office.

3 Make sure the journey follows a logical direction. This will preserve the order of the items on the list.

4 Once you are happy with your route, learn it before looking at the list. It could look something like this:

Stage	1	Front door
Stage	2	Gate
Stage	3	Corner shop
Stage	4	Traffic lights
Stage	5	Footbridge
Stage	6	Station entrance
Stage	7	Platform 4
Stage	8	Train
Stage	9	Church
Stage	10	College gates
Stage	11	Library
Stage	12	Your desk

The idea is to mentally place each item of the list opposite at each stage of the journey. For example, if the first stage of your chosen route is the front door, then imagine seeing a huge **bell** planted on your doorstep preventing you from leaving. Approaching the second stage, you see long strips of **bacon** draped over the gate as you sense that unmistakable smell wafting in the air – a very odd sight. Outside the corner shop you see the characteristic shape of the **Eiffel Tower**. It's only a model of the original, but what on earth is it doing there? … and so on.

Imagine journeying to college as you would on any other day, only this time you will experience some unusual encounters along the way. As well as visualising each item at each stage, try to conjure up the atmosphere of the location. Use all your senses – listen to the traffic; what's the weather like, mild or cold? Taste, smell and touch will play a part, and note your reactions as you see each item.

Tip: don't try to memorise the words, just try to bring them to life. Remember, this is a test of imagination. There is no time limit, so don't rush. Just enjoy the trip.

1 Bell
2 Bacon
3 Eiffel Tower
4 Michael Schumacher
5 Grease
6 Bob Geldof
7 Ice cream
8 Lux soap
9 Net
10 Glass of port
11 Bull
12 Crown

I said at the beginning that this was a test of imagination. However, as I believe imagination is the key to memory, I fully expect you to be able to recall all twelve items.

Total recall

To recall the list, all you have to do is review the journey. Play back your mental cine-film and reminisce over the unusual scenes.

If you did hit a blank at any stage it's not your memory that's defective, it's the way you programmed the information in the first place. Don't blame the projector when the recording equipment's at fault. If you missed a scene, then the picture you created obviously didn't make a big enough impact on your memory and was not sufficiently stimulating, so go back to the relevant location and reshoot that scene. You probably found it easier to remember the two people, Schumacher and Geldof, than some of the less animated items, for the reasons I've already given. That's why it's necessary to exaggerate the scenes to compensate for some of the less interesting items.

The beauty of this method is that it's so well organised – assuming, of course, that your route is. It is a highly effective mental filing system, allowing quick, easy access to any data required. For example, if you wanted to know what item comes after "bacon", you could pinpoint the answer, "Eiffel Tower", simply by referring to your route. Similarly, you could repeat the whole list backwards by reversing the journey – that is, by travelling back home from college.

Did you notice anything significant about the items themselves? Here's another lateral poser for you:

Question: What is the connection between each of the items?

Answer: They are symbols for the first twelve countries to join the European Union, which you have unwittingly been tricked into memorising in alphabetical order.

I should say that they are my symbols. Whenever you use this method you should create your own very personal symbolic representations. Even so, you should be able to see the connection from this list:

1 Belgium
2 Denmark
3 France
4 Germany
5 Greece
6 Ireland
7 Italy
8 Luxembourg
9 Netherlands
10 Portugal
11 Spain
12 United Kingdom

If you found that exercise easy, then there is no reason why you shouldn't start exploiting the journey method further. Using this method, the amount of knowledge that can be stored is virtually limitless, because the amount of storage space available – in geographical locations, for example – is essentially unlimited. I measure my own storage capacity by the amount of journeys or routes that I have gathered and organised over the past few years. In fact, I have about 100 journeys in my head, each consisting of fifty-two stages.

In theory, then, it's possible for me to memorise 5,200 playing cards (100 packs), or 5,200 names, faces, numbers – or anything else. But this is a conservative estimate because each stage could easily accommodate many more images. Think of your own route. If you used your desk at college as just one stage of the journey, imagine how many more images could be stored throughout the rest of the college buildings and grounds.

So my original figure of 5,200 is really more like 50,000 as far as storing "bits" of information goes; but if I were studying for exams I wouldn't be using this storage space to memorise sequences of numbers, football scores and racing results. I would be saturating my mental maps with historical events, Shakespearean quotations, foreign vocabularies, chemical formulae, maths equations, laws of physics, economic statistics, and so on.

In the coming chapters, I will be concentrating on the techniques that will enable you to achieve this for yourself.

Master discs and blank discs

I liken my journeys to video tapes or to rewritable DVDs, because they share similar characteristics. Once you have bought a blank video-cassette or disc, you can use it to record documentaries, films, sport, comedy, drama and so on, and you can use that same tape or disc to record on over and over again, *ad infinitum* according to the manufacturers. This is possible because every time you make a fresh recording, whatever was last recorded gets wiped off, and, unless you are hopelessly sentimental, this is a very handy facility. However, to retain your favourite film, you can create a master version by removing the bit of plastic from the back of the cassette or by "locking" the disc.

This is how I organise my own mental discs. I have about 100 journey-discs, of which fifty are blank. These I use for record attempts, demonstrations, memory competitions and everyday use. Because the sort of information I am memorising, like a 1,000-digit binary number, is not worthy of long-term storage, I can use these same journeys or discs over and over again. The new sequence simply wipes out or records over the old one.

The remaining fifty master discs I use for storing data like Number One hits, football championship winners – anything that needs to be kept for future reference.

Every so often, I play or review some of these old discs to refresh my memory, usually before a demonstration, and occasionally I need to update the information as things change, either by extending the journey or by adding further images to existing stages. Perhaps a better analogy in this case would be that of a computer file in which I can easily access the stored information, update it and save it for future use.

ANCIENT GREECE AND VIRTUAL JOURNEYS

The memory techniques I have just described are the product of my own trials, conducted over many years. Perhaps I should say trials and errors; some of my earlier methods were not always successful. Because these systems have been developed literally from scratch and independently over time, I had assumed that they were completely original. Indeed, having since compared my work with other books on memory, I have found that although many of them encourage the use of association, conversion of numbers into images (see chapter nine) and imagination, hardly any emphasis is placed on the use of locations.

I have always stressed that familiar locations are essential for anchoring all the mnemonically generated images (images you create in order to jog your memory). They provide order by acting as three-dimensional filing systems. Without places, images have nowhere to live, and so hang around in the air like lost souls. If images are left to float in a sort of fog, then they will be difficult to access, fade quickly from the memory, and be easily confused with other images, which rather makes the use of techniques for aiding memory pointless.

A time-honoured technique

However, my hopes of being the inventor of a revolutionary new method for enhancing memory were soon dashed after I learned that the ancient Greeks had already discovered these methods more than 2,000 years ago. To the

Greeks, memory was an art form, and they were masters of it. This is not surprising when you consider that they were living in a book-free age. Although a crude form of paper, papyrus, existed, and wax tablets were used occasionally for important texts, the ancient Greek tradition was truly oral. It was vitally important to have a good memory – we know that in Athens, school students were expected to learn Homer's epic poems the *Iliad* and the *Odyssey* by heart (that's equivalent to a book of about 800 pages in modern terms). If an individual did not possess a naturally good memory, it was necessary to develop an artificial one.

This skill was known as mnemotechnics. An unknown Roman teacher of rhetoric compiled one of the few ancient texts on the subject that remain: *Ad Herennium*. It is a treatise on the precise rules for training the memory, which preserved a tradition that began with the Greeks.

Practising the art of memory in the twenty-first century, as I do, can seem like a solitary pursuit, so it is somewhat comforting to learn that I'm not the only one to have taken extensive excursions through an internal, imaginary world. As the anonymous teacher says,

> *"If we wish to remember much material we must equip ourselves with a large number of places. It is essential that the places should form a series and must be remembered in their order, so that we can start in any place* [locus] *in the series and move either backward or forward from it."*

85

Here, the author is clearly affirming the use of the journey method you have just learned in this book to remember a list of information.

He goes on to say,

> "A locus *is a place easily grasped by the memory, such as a house, an intercolumnar space, a corner, an arch, or the like. If we wish to remember, for example, the genus of a horse, of a lion, of an eagle, we must place their images on definite* loci."

You may be tempted to think that you simply don't know enough locations to store all the information you need to remember for the academic courses you are following. But your imagination will ensure that you can never run out, because, as the ancient author says,

> "*Even a person who thinks he does not possess enough sufficiently good* loci *can remedy this. For thought can embrace any region whatsoever and in it and at will construct the setting of some place.*"

In other words, if you think about it, there is an infinite number of imaginary places that you could create in your mind to house your mnemonic images. The Greeks used a healthy mixture of fictitious places as well as real ones to boost their memory power. If there aren't enough rooms in your house to make a long enough route, you could always create an extra floor or dig out a basement block. Anything's possible.

Virtual journeys

At this point I have to admit to a passion for computer games. Apart from the entertainment I gain through the problem-solving they require, games offer a certain escapist value, as the illusion created by the graphics is powerful enough to give one some sense of "being there". However, these are not completely idle pursuits; I use the geography of the virtual worlds of some computer games as the basis for some of my mental journeys.

Surprisingly, they seem to be no less effective than real locations when it comes to storing information. So the next time you are caught at the computer when you're supposed to be studying, you'll have a legitimate excuse. Just say you're swotting up on *Hamlet* – and if your accuser doesn't believe you, tell them to read this!

9   The Language of Numbers

> *"When you have mastered numbers, you will in fact no longer be reading numbers, any more than you read words when reading books. You will be reading meanings."*
> — W.E.B. Du Bois (1868–1963)

MNEMONICS

The reason I am able to memorise long sequences of random numbers, binary digits and playing cards is because I have spent the past few years perfecting a technique using mnemonics. What are these?

A mnemonic is any device that aids memory. The name is derived from Mnemosyne, the Greek goddess of memory, who, after spending nine consecutive nights with Zeus (allegedly), gave birth to the nine Muses. Mnemonics are extremely useful for converting seemingly unintelligible data into a more intelligible form which the brain can then accept and make use of.

In this chapter I will reveal the precise mechanics of that process, which I hope, once adopted, you will utilise in passing exams and not for cleaning up at the card tables!

The difficulty with numbers

It seems that no matter what subject you are studying, at some point or other numbers, in whatever form, are presented to you and you must remember them. Wouldn't studying be so much more palatable if we didn't have to worry about dates, equations, formulae, sums and economic statistics? It's as though they're thrown in periodically to deliberately slow us down and disrupt our flow of learning. But without them our lives would be chaotic. Numbers are everywhere and we have to deal with them on a daily basis. Credit cards, telephone numbers, gas bills, appointments, bus timetables, exam results … everything has to be quantified, reckoned, tallied, and so numeracy counts.

The difficulty with numbers is that, seen in isolation, they have very little meaning. The sequence 13, 10, 79, 82 is hardly a memorable run of numbers, but if you were told that these were the amounts of money, in thousands, that you were going to inherit over the next four years, those numbers would suddenly possess a resonance all of their own. Numbers are difficult to grasp because they are intangible, faceless creatures with no individual personalities. It's little wonder that when we are tested, their abstract nature prevents most of us from being able to recall more than eight or nine digits from any given sequence.

Speaking of numbers …

One of the most gruelling and nerve-racking events of the World Memory Championships is the spoken number test. Contestants have to memorise a long, random sequence of numbers, which is fed to them verbally at a consistent rate of one digit per second. The sequence must then be recalled and the numbers written down. Scores are calculated by the number of digits the contestant can recall correctly before a mistake is made. Sudden death, in other words.

Only a few years ago, my score would probably have been seven, which is about average for a test like this, but by using a system I managed to extend this to 128. The current record held for the competition is 198 digits! The reason I was able to achieve my best of 128 is because I made the unintelligible world of numbers intelligible. My method gives to numbers what they were lacking in the first place – their own unique characters.

Each pair of digits, and there are 100 of them ranging from 00 to 99, represents a person to me, each one carrying out his or her own unique activity. For example, when I see the number 15 I think of Einstein, while the number 48 represents British racing driver Damon Hill – the first of these is always chalking a blackboard in my mind, and the second, of course, driving a Formula One car.

Question: Why does the number 15 = Einstein?

Answer: because the first and fifth letters of the alphabet are A and E, Albert Einstein's initials.

This process of translating numbers into letters and then letters into people is central to the method I have christened the DOMINIC System, which could stand for either:

- *The Deciphering Of Mnemonically Interpreted Numbers Into Characters*

  or

- *The Decoding Of Mundane Incoherent Numbers Into Clarity!*

It's like learning a new language, but as the vocabulary only consists of 100 words it doesn't take long to master. Once you are fluent you will soon see the many practical advantages this system has to offer.

Before I reveal the nuts and bolts of this new language, there are a couple of basic systems which are easy to acquire and very useful for memorising things like positions, quantities and short lists.

RHYMING NUMBERS

The number–rhyme is a method popular among magicians for memorising the order of a sequence of objects. It's a very simple, basic method but can be used in a variety of practical ways.

It works this way: first think of a word that rhymes with a number. For example, you might choose "door" to rhyme with the number four. The door then becomes what is known as your key image for that number, which you can use to associate with the fourth item of whatever list you need to memorise.

It has been observed time and time again that for a system like this to work effectively, it is the student who should create his or her own associations. I can explain the principles of a system and advance what I feel are the most efficient ways of applying them, but the world of the imagination is a uniquely personal one, so it's always best to use your own ideas.

However, if you're not feeling very creative, here are some suggestions of possible number–rhymes:

1   Gun, bun
2   Shoe, loo
3   Tree, bee
4   Door, saw
5   Hive, dive
6   Sticks, bricks
7   Heaven, Kevin
8   Gate, date
9   Wine, sign
10 Pen, den

Once you have decided on your own personal number–rhymes, you're ready to apply them, so here's a simple exercise to get you started. Try memorising the order of the last ten British Prime Ministers. It's easy. All you have to do is imagine each person in the list interacting with his or her corresponding key image, and the correct order will be fixed in your brain. It doesn't matter if you've never heard some of these names before, or know what they look like. The point is that even for the most unlikely information, an image can be created to link it with a number.

For example, for John Major you could imagine a military major wearing a huge, shiny **shoe**, or sitting on the **loo**! Similarly for the other people on the list, simply use the name, or part of the name, to trigger an associated or substitute image – for example, a mackintosh for Macmillan, a thatched cottage for Margaret Thatcher, or your own front door with a big AD written on it for Alec Douglas-Home. Although Harold Wilson served twice, you should find it no problem linking him into a couple of wild scenes to connect him to the numbers five and seven. Remember to use all your senses, as well as adding movement and exaggeration to the scenes and let your imagination go for it. Allow yourself three minutes at the most.

1   Tony Blair
2   John Major
3   Margaret Thatcher
4   James Callaghan
5   Harold Wilson
6   Edward Heath
7   Harold Wilson
8   Alec Douglas-Home
9   Harold Macmillan
10 Anthony Eden

Now, without referring to the list, fill in the correct Prime Minister next to the corresponding positional number.

7 _____

6 _____

3 _____

2 _____

8 _____

9 _____

1 _____

10 _____

5 _____

4 _____

Apart from the practical benefits of using a system like this, the fact that you are stretching your imagination is a great exercise for toning up those "memory muscles". You will find that the more you practise these exercises, the easier they will become. Just as with any other muscle in the body, the more you use it, the stronger it gets.

NUMBER–SHAPES

If you tend to think more in images than in words, as I do, then you might find that this method suits you better.

The number–shape is an alternative method to the number–rhyme, only this time you create your key image from the physical shape of the number. For example, what does the shape of the number 7 remind you of? The edge of

HOW TO PASS EXAMS

a cliff, a kerbstone or maybe a boomerang? The number 4 reminds me of the shape of a sailboat and the number 2, a swan. Draw up your own list of shapes for the numbers 1 to 10 but again, if you're short on ideas, here's a selection to choose from:

1 Candle, pole
2 Swan, snake
3 Handcuffs, lips
4 Sailboat, flag
5 Curtain hook, seahorse
6 Elephant's trunk, mallet
7 Boomerang, diving board
8 Egg timer, female model
9 Balloon and string, monocle
10 Hoop and stick, Laurel and Hardy

The number–shape method can be used as an alternative to, or in combination with, number–rhymes for memorising a varied range of data. You used the number–rhyme method to learn the order of British Prime Ministers, but it can also be used, as can number–shapes, for remembering quantity.

For example, to remind you that there are nine major planets, you could picture a huge balloon and string encapsulating the entire solar system. And the surreal image of a beautiful white swan gracefully flapping its wings as it endlessly orbits Mars is a reminder of how many moons that planet has – two. This is an extremely efficient method for absorbing massive amounts of information, no matter how

obscure or trivial the detail; and because the images created are so bizarre and exaggerated, they leave a long-lasting impression on the memory. This, then, is surely a valuable tool to employ when cramming for exams. I myself have used it to help me remember over 7,500 answers to Trivial Pursuit questions.

This time, use your own number-shapes to link the following questions to their numerical answers:

Question	Answer
How many sides does a snowflake have?	6
A cow's stomach has how many compartments?	4
How many colours are there in the spectrum?	7
The Titanic went down with how many funnels?	4
How many hearts does an octopus have?	3
How many wings does a bee have?	4
How many equal angles does an isosceles triangle have?	2

Once you've created your images, fill in the missing numbers below:

A bee has __ wings.

A snowflake has __ sides.

There are __ colours in the spectrum.

There are __ equal angles in an isosceles triangle.

The Titanic had __ funnels.

An octopus has __ hearts.

A cow's stomach has __ compartments.

There are __ planets in the solar system.

Test yourself tomorrow, and again in one week's time. If the mental pictures you have just created were sufficiently stimulating, you may well find you are stuck with these trivial facts permanently!

THE DOMINIC SYSTEM

I originally designed the DOMINIC System for competitions. I wanted a method that would allow me to recognise numbers as images as soon as I saw them. I thought that by familiarising myself with groups of numbers, I would literally be able to read through and make sense of a number with 100 digits in the same way that I am able to read through and understand a sentence composed of 100 letters divided into words.

I toyed with the idea of drawing up a table of set images for all four-digit permutations – a lampstand might represent the number 8,047, or a goat the number 5,564. But there are 10,000 combinations of four-digit numbers, which means I would never have the time to familiarise myself with each item. Even three-digit numbers proved too big a vocabulary. But pairs of digits were manageable.

I had learned from card memorisation that the most successful key images were people rather than objects. People are flexible, mobile and they react. Shout abuse at or pay compliments to a lampstand and it won't flinch, but a person will. So every pair of numbers is a person to me.

Some numbers are easy to convert into people. You might associate 07 with James Bond and 99 with an ice cream vendor. I link 39 with the memory man from the Alfred Hitchcock film *The Thirty-nine Steps*; and 57 with my godfather (as 1957 was the year I was born). If you start thinking about it, you should find that you can make a connection, no matter how tenuous, with many numbers.

However, for numbers with which you can't forge an immediate link, you'll need to build mental stepping stones to help guide you to your key character image. An easy way to do this is to associate each digit with a letter of the alphabet (see below). You can then combine pairs of letters to create the initials for people, as I explain on pages 100–105.

The letters of the DOMINIC System
You need to create a system that makes sense to you, and commit it to memory. I use the following basic set of letters:

$$1 = A$$
$$2 = B$$
$$3 = C$$
$$4 = D$$
$$5 = E$$
$$6 = S \text{ (the first letter of "six")}$$
$$7 = G$$
$$8 = H$$
$$9 = N \text{ (the first letter of "nine")}$$
$$0 = O \text{ (due to the similar shapes)}$$

These letters are merely a key for converting numbers into meaningful images, so feel free to invent your own set.

Once you have learnt your set of letters, you can start to pair letters together to form the initials of various people. Your cast should include a rich mixture of friends, enemies, relatives, actors, singers, comedians, celebrities, cartoon characters and historically famous people. It's not necessary to be able to form a vivid mental picture of each person, but a vague impression of a physical feature or characteristic action will greatly help. I have found that it's not so much someone's physical appearance that leaves a lasting image in my memory, as their personality shining through.

Building your cast of characters

If you can't associate the number 48, for example, with any-one directly, take the corresponding letters, DH, to form a person's initials: Damon Hill, Debbie Harry or Daryl Hannah. Similarly, 16 becomes AS, which could translate into Arnold Schwarzenegger.

Of course, the letters don't always have to match the initials of the person you've chosen. If NO (90) makes you think of your father because that's what he's always telling you and CD (34) of your sister because she is always playing CDs, then use them as your key images for these numbers.

Here are a few guidelines to help build up your army of memory aid-workers.

1 Draw up a list of 100 numbers from 00 to 99, and then start filling in the names of all the people for whom you have immediate associations.

2   When you have exhausted this avenue, decode the numbers into letters and see whose initials fit.

3   Try to make your army of people as diverse and colourful as possible. You must be able to distinguish between characters, so, for example, try to have only one footballer, guitarist or golfer in your list.

4   Each person should be accompanied by his or her own prop or action. In my list Eric Clapton (EC = 53) is always playing and carrying his guitar, while Bob Dylan (BD = 24) is always playing the harmonica. This distinguishing feature is not just important for making the characters more memorable; as you will see later, when you memorise longer numbers, people and actions can be made interchangeable.

5   If you set yourself a target of twenty people a day, by the end of the week you will have learned a new language.

6   Familiarise yourself with the list. Get to know your characters by testing yourself whenever you have a dull moment – on a bus, in the bath or last thing at night. It's a practical alternative to counting sheep!

As I have always stressed, your own associations are the most memorable ones, but the following cast of characters with their associated actions are the ones I use and they might help to plug the odd gap where you're having trouble thinking of someone. These are the people I'll be using as examples through the rest of the book:

00	OO	Olive Oyl	Eating spinach
01	OA	Ossie Ardiles	Playing football
02	OB	Orlando Bloom	Shooting an arrow
03	OC	Oliver Cromwell	Loading a musket
04	OD	Otto Dix	Painting
05	OE	Old Etonian	Wearing a boater
06	OS	Omar Sharif	Playing backgammon
07	OG	Organ Grinder	Holding monkey
08	OH	Oliver Hardy	Wearing bowler hat
09	ON	Old Nick	In hell
10	AO	Annie Oakley	Shooting guns
11	AA	Andre Agassi	Playing tennis
12	AB	Anne Boleyn	Being beheaded
13	AC	Al Capone	Smoking cigar
14	AD	The Artful Dodger	Picking a pocket
15	AE	Albert Einstein	Chalking a blackboard
16	AS	Arnold Schwarzenegger	Flexing muscles
17	AG	Alec Guinness	Drinking Guinness
18	AH	Adolf Hitler	Goose-stepping
19	AN	Alfred Nobel	Giving prizes
20	BO	Bill Oddie	Holding binoculars
21	BA	Ben Affleck	Kissing Jennifer Lopez
22	BB	Bugs Bunny	Eating a carrot
23	BC	Bill Clinton	Waving US flag
24	BD	Bob Dylan	Playing harmonica
25	BE	Brian Epstein	Playing records
26	BS	Britney Spears	Wrestling with snake
27	BG	Bob Geldof	Being knighted

28	BH	Benny Hill	Driving milk float
29	BN	Barry Norman	Watching a film
30	CO	Chris O'Donnell	Helping Batman
31	CA	Charlie's Angels	Flicking their hair
32	CB	Chuck Berry	Doing the duck walk
33	CC	Charlie Chaplin	Bending cane
34	CD	Charles Darwin	Catching butterflies
35	CE	Clint Eastwood	Lassoing
36	CS	Claudia Schiffer	Striding along catwalk
37	CG	Che Guevara	Holding machine gun
38	CH	Charlton Heston	Riding in a chariot
39	CN	Chuck Norris	Doing a karate kick
40	DO	Dominic O'Brien	Reciting numbers
41	DA	David Attenborough	Crawling in bush
42	DB	David Bowie	Putting on make-up
43	DC	Daniel Craig	Playing poker
44	DD	Donald Duck	Quacking
45	DE	Duke Ellington	Playing piano
46	DS	Delia Smith	Baking a cake
47	DG	David Gower	Using a cricket bat
48	DH	Damon Hill	Racing car
49	DN	David Niven	Wearing dinner jacket
50	EO	Eeyore	Chewing thistles
51	EA	Emperor Augustus	Wearing a toga
52	EB	Enid Blyton	Writing a book
53	EC	Eric Clapton	Playing guitar
54	ED	Eliza Doolittle	Selling flowers
55	EE	Edna Everage	Waving gladioli

56	ES	Ebenezer Scrooge	Counting money
57	EG	Edvard Grieg	Conducting orchestra
58	EH	Edmund Hillary	At top of Everest
59	EN	Emperor Nero	Playing the violin
60	SO	Scarlett O'Hara	Fainting
61	SA	Salvador Allende	Eating a chilli (Chile)
62	SB	Sleeping Beauty	Sleeping
63	SC	Sean Connery	Holding a gun
64	SD	Salvador Dali	With huge moustache
65	SE	Sue Ellen	Drinking vodka
66	SS	Steven Spielberg	Pointing, with ET
67	SG	The Spice Girls	Eating a curry
68	SH	Saddam Hussein	Burning oil wells
69	SN	Sam Neill	Running from dinosaur
70	GO	George Orwell	Fighting off rats
71	GA	Georgio Armani	Dressmaking
72	GB	George Bush	Burning a bush
73	GC	George Clooney	Wearing stethoscope
74	GD	Gérard Depardieu	Wielding sword
75	GE	George Eliot	Writing a novel
76	GS	Gilbert & Sullivan	Performing opera
77	GG	Germaine Greer	Burning a bra
78	GH	George Harrison	Meditating
79	GN	Greg Norman	Playing golf
80	HO	Hazel O'Connor	Breaking glass
81	HA	Harold Abrams	Running
82	HB	Humphrey Bogart	Wearing mac and hat
83	HC	Henry Cooper	Boxing

84	HD	Humpty Dumpty	Falling off wall
85	HE	Harry Enfield	Making a 'phone call
86	HS	Homer Simpson	Eating doughnuts
87	HG	Hugh Grant	Getting married
88	HH	Hulk Hogan	Wrestling
89	HN	Horatio Nelson	Manning the helm
90	NO	Nick Owen	Sitting on a sofa
91	NA	Neil Armstrong	Wearing a spacesuit
92	NB	Norman Bates	Taking a shower
93	NC	Naomi Campbell	Tripping over
94	ND	Neil Diamond	Sitting on rocks
95	NE	Noel Edmonds	Opening a box
96	NS	Nancy Sinatra	Duetting with Frank
97	NG	Noel Gallagher	Singing into a "mike"
98	NH	Nasser Hussein	Bowling a cricket ball
99	NN	Nick Nolte	Dressed as a tramp

Remember that your own ideas will work much better for you. Remember also that the letters are merely acting as an intermediary stage, bridging the gap between intangible digits and tangible images. This conversion process will seem a bit slow in the early stages because, as your brain is learning a new skill, it has to work step by step through several stages of thought.

- *Initial learning steps:*
  numbers → letters → initials → name → person → image

However, with a little practice, you will soon be able to leap those steps by automatically seeing a number as a person.

- *Reflexive stage:*
  numbers → image

When a trained pianist sight-reads from a score of music, he or she doesn't have to convert each note into a letter and then work out its position on the keyboard. Enough practice has ensured that the fingers know instinctively where to go. The same will be true for you with the DOMINIC System once you have had enough practice.

HOW TO USE YOUR NEW LANGUAGE

You have already seen how number–rhymes and number–shapes can be used to remember data involving single or double digits. But by combining those methods with the DOMINIC System you will have a multifaceted weapon for tackling any combination of numbers, no matter how long the sequence.

Three-digit numbers

To remember any three-digit number, you divide the number into a pair of digits followed by a single digit. For example, 236 would become 23 and 6. By combining the DOMINIC System with the number–shape method this would give you the image of Bill Clinton (BC = 23) riding an elephant (number shape for 6). The number 433 would become 43 and 3, which produces Daniel Craig (DC = 43) handcuffed (number shape for 3). This combination of two key images produces what I shall refer to from now on as a **complex** image.

Four-digit numbers

I said before that it was important for each person to carry out a unique action or have a unique prop, as these could be made interchangeable.

Let's take the number 1,846, which can be split into 18 and 46. By referring to the list, this gives us two people: Adolf Hitler (AH = 18) and cookery guru Delia Smith (DS = 46). This time, however, we take the **action** of Delia Smith and give it to Adolf Hitler. In other words, to remember 1,846 you would form the unlikely complex image of the Führer baking a cake.

18	46
Adolf Hitler	*baking a cake*
(person)	*(action)*

What if the numbers were switched to form 4,618? In this case the roles are simply reversed: you would imagine Delia Smith goose-stepping! Hitler's physical presence is no longer required; only his mannerisms remain.

46	18
Delia Smith	*goose-stepping*
(person)	*(action)*

Five-digit numbers and above

As you can see, pairs of numbers work like mental hooks, linking into each other. To memorise a longer sequence, you keep adding further hooks to form a mental chain.

As a general rule, I always work from left to right, slicing the number into pairs of person–action/person–action, and so on; and if there is one digit remaining, then this will be a number–shape. Take the number 35,774. First arrange the digits into 35, 77 and 4, then translate them into person, action and number–shape. Using my list, you should end up with the absurd complex image of Clint Eastwood burning a bra on a boat.

35	77	4
Clint Eastwood	*burning bra*	*sailboat*
(person)	*(action)*	*(number–shape)*

Again, although the key character for 77 is feminist writer Germaine Greer (GG = 77), we only require her associated action, bra-burning. And, remember, the action always takes place in or near your number–shape, in this case, a sailboat.

With six-digit numbers you imagine a person performing an action on or in the company of another person, which can get very interesting. The number 724,268 gives the complex image of George Bush putting make-up on Saddam Hussein. How about 159,267? This gives you Albert Einstein having a shower with the Spice Girls. But my favourite is 408,836, as it translates into Dominic O'Brien wrestling with Claudia Schiffer.

40	88	36
Dominic O'Brien	*wrestling*	*Claudia Schiffer*
(person)	*(action)*	*(person)*

I'm sure that after just a short while working with this system you, too, will find your favourite numbers.

SUMMARY

- The best way to remember numbers is to breathe life into them by giving them an artificial meaning, a personality, a set of characteristics.

- The DOMINIC System works like a dictionary, translating foreign, unintelligible digits into more meaningful, memorable images.

- Create your own cast of characters by drawing up a list from 00 to 99. Gradually fill in the names of people you associate with certain numbers, and make sure you highlight a unique characteristic action for each.

- The language is easy, quick and fun to learn. You won't need to travel abroad to pick up the lingo, as numbers are everywhere and, because you are in contact with them on a daily basis, you will have ample opportunity to practise and become fluent.

- Once you are fluent – and it won't take long – you will be able to start munching your way through huge chunks of numerical data with a degree of zeal. Just as anyone who has been studying French can't wait to practise their new tongue in a Parisian café, so you, too, will relish the thought of absorbing history dates, statistics and figures. Once they were there to make you yawn and slow you down, but soon they'll be a welcome break.

10　Never Forget a Quotation

"The best books are those whose readers think
they could have written them."

— Blaise Pascal (1623–62)

PREPARING YOURSELF

If you are studying English literature or training for the dramatic arts, this is the chapter for you. In English literature you can expect to sit one or more of three types of examination: open book, unprepared text or closed book. In open book exams, you are allowed to take your own text into the exam and you can refer to your own handwritten margin notes. For this type of exam you must have a thorough knowledge of the text and its context, as it is your understanding, commentary and analysis that are being tested.

If your literature exam involves passages of unprepared text, you will need to rely on your understanding of literary techniques to write a response to the text, but at least you have the words in front of you – no problems of forgetting characters' names or key themes and how they are related.

In closed book exams, however, you are not afforded the luxury of seeing any text, and under these conditions you must be able to produce short quotations from memory, as well as providing evidence that you have a clear insight into the work itself. You will not be expected to quote at great length, but having key lines of poetry, phrases of prose or dramatic speeches fixed confidently in your mind will enable you to support your points with speed, assurance and skill – which will impress examiners no end.

In this chapter I will outline a simple method for learning quotes similar to a very successful one used by the Greeks and Romans, and by some actors today. It can dramatically cut down the amount of time you devote purely to arduous rote learning, allowing more time to get on with the job of interpreting a text's meaning. If you are taking a course in theatre studies or performing arts, you will find this method invaluable for learning lines for performance as well as for exams.

The process of memorising poetry, prose or lines from plays should be a joy, not a burden. It's not only the pleasure that's removed by repetition of a line *ad infinitum*; the significance and appeal of the words can also get lost as they dissolve into a bland, rhythmically predictable singsong. This is why I'm reluctant to play some of my favourite CDs too often, lest their attraction should be spoiled by overkill.

If you remember words produced from images rather than relying purely on the sounds made by your tongue, you will have a richer appreciation of the literature you are studying, longer retention of it and a greater, more significant comprehension of its meaning.

In chapter eleven, I will show you how to learn a basic foreign vocabulary by mentally placing key images in a familiar town or village. You won't be surprised to find that to remember quotes you'll need to adopt a similar method. As always, the three essential, inseparable components of this method are imagination, association and location.

Remembering short quotes

There are a number of ways to store individual quotes or separate lines of poetry ready for deployment in an exam. The best way is to "house" them all in a certain building or contained area in the same way that you will house foreign vocabulary in certain parts of town in chapter eleven and chemical elements around your school or college in chapter thirteen. As it's the written word we're dealing with, you could store them in your local library or bookshop. In some cases, a single image attached to an object, piece of furniture or special feature in the building may be enough to trigger off the memory of a whole quote.

What would your key image be to remind you of the opening line of Shakespeare's *Twelfth Night*?

- *"If music be the food of love, play on …"*

Mine is a heart-shaped chocolate guitar. Positioned at the entrance of my local bookshop, music is wafting from the guitar, luring in passers-by.

- *"… To die, to sleep.*
  To sleep, perchance to dream. Ay, there's the rub …"

How would you remember this famous line-and-a-half and that it occurs in Act III, scene 1 of *Hamlet*?

I would imagine the area around the cash tills as a stage. The curtain rises to reveal Charlie's Angels (CA = 31), who are rubbing tears from their eyes. They are grieving at the sight of a dead man who appears to be asleep. Notice how this time I have combined III and 1 to give me the number 31. You should decide for yourself how best to use the systems I have outlined for converting numbers into images (see chapter nine); then combine your number image with the information you need to memorise.

Now try to memorise the following quotations and short literary extracts by translating them into what for you is the most direct symbolic imagery. Remember, as ever, to enrich your images by bringing into play as much of the following as you can: all your senses (touch, taste, sight, smell, sound), motion, emotion, sexuality, colour, association, substitution, exaggeration, humour, symbolism and – most important of all – imagination. Don't forget to house the images somewhere so that you have a backdrop. For an exam, you could house quotes by different authors in different locations.

"*Through the Jungle very softly flits a Shadow and a sigh –*
He is Fear, O Little Hunter, he is fear!"
Rudyard Kipling (1865–1936), *The Song of the Little Hunter*

"*The roots of education are bitter, but the fruit is sweet.*"
Aristotle (384–322BCE)

"*Tyger! Tyger! burning bright*
  In the forests of the night,
  What immortal hand or eye
  Could frame thy fearful symmetry?"
William Blake (1757–1827), *Songs of Innocence and
of Experience*

"*We were alone with the quiet day, and his little heart,*
  dispossessed, had stopped."
Henry James (1843–1916), *The Turn of the Screw*

"*Here's the smell of the blood still; all the perfumes of*
  Arabia will not sweeten / this little hand."
William Shakespeare (1564–1616), *Macbeth* V.1

Remembering a lengthy speech

Some dramatic speeches are so important to an understanding of themes, character and plot that it is worth
knowing them in their entirety. The example I am going to
use is an extract from Shakespeare's *Hamlet* given to me by
a student who was having difficulty trying to memorise it.

ACT I SCENE 2

O that this too too solid flesh would melt,
Thaw, and resolve itself into a dew,   130
Or that the Everlasting had not fix'd
His canon 'gainst self-slaughter! O God, O God,
How weary, stale, flat, and unprofitable
Seem to me all the uses of this world!
Fie on't, ah fie, fie! 'Tis an unweeded garden,
That grows to seed; things rank and gross in nature
Possess it merely. That it should come to this –
But two months dead – nay, not so much, not two –
So excellent a king, that was to this
Hyperion to a satyr, so loving to my mother   140
That he might not beteem the winds of heaven
Visit her face too roughly! Heaven and earth,
Must I remember? Why, she would hang on him
As if increase of appetite had grown
By what it fed on, and yet within a month –
Let me not think on't; frailty, thy name is woman –
A little month, or ere those shoes were old
With which she follow'd my poor father's body,
Like Niobe, all tears, why she, even she –
O God, a beast, that wants discourse of reason   150
Would have mourn'd longer – married with mine uncle,
My father's brother, but no more like my father
Than I to Hercules; within a month,
Ere yet the salt of most unrighteous tears
Had left the flushing of her galled eyes,

She married. O most wicked speed, to post
With such dexterity to incestuous sheets!
It is not, nor it cannot come to good.
But break, my heart, for I must hold my tongue.   159

This particular soliloquy contains thirty-one lines. So if you wanted to commit this to memory for an exam or performance, the best way would be to take a mental journey consisting of thirty-one stages. To learn a foreign vocabulary, you place your key images in various places around a town as each word comes up at random. But as these lines are presented in a fixed order, your journey must possess a logical set sequence to protect the natural order of the words.

   When I'm memorising poetry I find that the best locations are ones situated in open spaces. Because there are several words on each line, you are going to need enough room to spread out the key images formed for each stage of your journey. A city or built-up area may be too congested, with far too many distractions obscuring or confusing these images. As suggested by the anonymous Roman author of *Ad Herennium* – a work we have already encountered in chapter eight (see pages 85–86):

> "*It is better to form one's memory loci in a deserted and solitary place, for crowds of passing people tend to weaken the impressions.*"

If you are a golfer like me, the layout of your local course will serve as an excellent location. The sequence of holes   117 will provide a natural path for your journey, the tees, fairways and greens acting as progressive stages along the way. Or you could use a favourite walk, preferably one in the countryside, that you knew as a child or make regularly now. Note interesting or significant landmarks along the way as you take a gentle stroll down your memory lane, counting them off as you go. Once you have thirty-one stages in your journey and know them back to front, you are ready to absorb the entire soliloquy.

Let's assume that you are already familiar with the play, maybe even to the extent of being able to recite individual lines. The problem is that you can't manage to string them together and get them to flow because you keep forgetting the order, or you get a mental block – a chronic problem for some budding thespians. All you need in this situation is a simple cue for each line in the form of a symbolic prompt.

Hamlet, as we know, is distraught to the point of suicide over the murder of his father and his evil uncle's marriage to his mother. Leaving this aside for the moment, concentrate on finding key symbols for the first few lines:

- *Stage 1:*
  "O that this too too solid flesh would melt,"

The idea is to convert the first word of each line into a key symbolic image and then mentally "place" it along one stage of the journey. Picture yourself at the start of your walk and imagine a big ring or hoop standing in front of you. This will then always serve as a reliable cue for O, the

118

NEVER FORGET A QUOTATION

first word of the first line. To remind you of the line itself, choose a suitable key image which you think best represents it – in this case, melting flesh.

My starting position is the first tee at East Herts golf club, where I imagine walking through a tall ring of fire as my right foot sinks into a pile of flesh that is melting from the heat. This scene, morbid as it is, will always remind me of the opening line.

- *Stage 2:*
  "Thaw, and resolve itself into a dew,"

At the second stage of your walk, use whatever your association for the word "thaw" might be to form the next line prompter, such as snow or thunder. On the first fairway I picture Thor, the Norse god of thunder, holding a glass of Resolve; a big dewdrop hangs off the end of his nose.

- *Stage 3:*
  "Or that the Everlasting had not fix'd"

Moving on to the third stage, create more symbols making "Or" the most prominent one. I see an oar sticking out of the hole on the green. Just beyond that is Eve, a friend, fixing something.

- *Stage 4:*
  "His canon 'gainst self-slaughter! O God, O God,"

Although the text relates to God's law (canon), it's easier to imagine a cannon and, in this case, one that self-destructs.

Watching the explosion is a pair of gods, or are you suffering from double vision? This scene, of course, takes place at the fourth stage of your journey.

Only you can judge how many key images you will need to form at each step of your journey in order to remember the whole line. It may even pay you to make up a mnemonic for every single word if you're starting to learn a piece from scratch.

- *Stage 5:*

  "How weary, stale, flat, and unprofitable"

With a little practice, you'll be able to find an association for any word. These are mine; your ideas may be different:

How	Apache Indian
weary	clothes rack
stale	bread with curled edge
flat	spirit level
and	Andrew
unprofitable	professor under the table

I said that it was preferable to use wide open spaces to allow enough room for your images to spread, and now you can see why. Once the words have been transformed into tangible images, they too can be joined together using the link method, and anchored to their particular stage.

But does all this really work? Yes – and for good reasons. You'll notice that because the images you create are so striking, and therefore memorable, you will be able to:

1 keep moving through the text as you are learning it without having to return so frequently to re-read, as you would if trying to memorise it by verbal repetition

2 retain the images, and therefore the words, far longer than you would by remembering the rhythm of the words alone.

The journey ensures that you always stay on track, and the individual stops along the way make it impossible for you ever to jump a section, miss out a line or lose the order.

The key images act as guide ropes or stepping stones enabling you to steer a smooth course through each line from word to word. As the Roman orator Cicero said,

> "*Memory for words, which for us is essential, is given distinctness by a greater variety of images, for there are many words which serve as joints connecting the limbs of a sentence … of these we have to model images for constant employment; but a memory for things is the special property of the orator – this we can imprint on our minds by a skilful arrangement of the several masks* [singulis personis] *that represent them, so that we may grasp ideas by means of **images** and their **order** by means of **places**."*

— Cicero, *De Oratore* (emphases are mine)

Once you are really familiar with the text, the mnemonic symbols will always be there to protect you from mental blocks by acting as three-dimensional idiot boards. The images will stick out in your mind, preventing you from "drying up".

After a while you will naturally gain a strong verbal recollection of the speech, guided by metre, cadence and rhythm. Although learning it line by line is the easiest way to memorise it, it necessarily divides the sense up artificially. Within a short time, though, the speech will flow so naturally that you will hardly notice your mnemonic journey – you'll be on "autopilot" – and the meaning of the speech, rather than just the words, will begin to emerge. However, should your "autopilot" let you down at any point, being able to see the words means you can always take over to fill any verbal gaps and keep yourself in full flight.

What's my line?

The method described above is particularly beneficial if you are an actor. As you can see all the lines of your part in the script laid out in front of your mind's eye, you'll know exactly how much space there is between other cast members' lines and your own; and this gives you time to prepare for your cue, as well as perfect synchronisation with everyone else. It's as though you are carrying a real script around with you all the time.

You can also pinpoint the exact position of a line by a simple calculation. If you make a mental note of every fifth or tenth stage along the route, you will quickly be able to work out the number of any particular line. I usually arrange it so that there is a door on the twenty-first stage on my route, and stairs with a sharp incline at the eleventh stage. For example, to find out what the twenty-second line is, you would picture stage 20 of your journey and then go forward by two stops. For immediate access to the twenty-ninth line, you would mentally walk back one stage from the thirtieth stage.

The soliloquy of Hamlet's that we have been looking at starts on line 129. To remember this, you could apply the DOMINIC System to provide a marker. By breaking the number of the line down into 12 – 9, I arrive at the complex image of Anne Boleyn (AB = 12) holding a balloon and string (number-shape for 9). Now, if you fuse this image to the first stage of your walk you will be able to quote any line at will thereafter, assuming of course that you have numbered a few intervals along the way.

- *What is line 131 Act I, scene II of* Hamlet?

A quick calculation tells you that the answer must lodge at the third stage of your journey, where you will again encounter the oar and immediately quote, "Or that the Everlasting had not fix'd ...".

- *What is line 158?*

Again, you can deduce that this must be stage 30 of your journey, or the last line but one, "It is not, nor it cannot come to good."

This is how I am able to "recite" the order of a pack of playing cards. By giving every card a mnemonic symbol and then placing them at predetermined intervals along an imaginary walk, I know precisely where each card is located along with the exact sequence. What people find most baffling, though, is the apparent ease with which I can give the numerical position – such as the fourteenth or twenty-sixth – of any card they nominate. But now you know the secret!

The language of Shakespeare

As all living languages evolve over time, so the meanings of words change. The word "silly" used to mean holy, and to "doubt" something meant that you had good reason to believe in it. To be able to interpret Shakespeare's plays fully, you will need to learn the meaning of certain phrases or individual words. There are several good study guides available on the market for all levels of examination.

To link interpretation to the words of the speech, simply add a new element to your key image for the line. For example, in the first line of the speech, Hamlet expresses his desire to commit suicide:

- *"O, that this too too solid flesh would melt"*

Modify the image at the first stage of your journey so that when you see the melting pile of flesh the effect is so revolting that you look away – only to notice someone standing on the ledge of a building ready to jump.

In the second line, the word "resolve" means "dissolve"

in modern terms; simple – just picture the god Thor's Resolve fizzing as it dissolves in the glass of water.

By now, you should know Hamlet's soliloquy well, and the muscles of your imagination should be exercised enough to create some links to remind you of the following interpretations of words and phrases in the speech.

- *canon 'gainst self-slaughter*
  God's law forbidding suicide

- *merely*
  fully, completely

- *Hyperion*
  sun god

- *satyr*
  half-human, half-goat

- *Hyperion to a satyr*
  contrast like chalk and cheese

- *beteem*
  permit, allow

- *visit*
  blow against

- *Niobe*
  heroine turned into stone as she wept for her children

- *wants discourse of reason*
  is not capable of rational thought

- *unrighteous tears*
  false, crocodile tears

- *to post*
  to hurry

- *dexterity*
  speed

Study tips

It is your understanding, interpretation and opinions that are going to be tested in the final reckoning, so it is very much in your own interest to take as much of an active role as possible when studying a play.

Put yourself in the shoes of each character. Imagine what it must be like for Hamlet. How would you react to your mother marrying your uncle less than two months after he'd taken your father's life? Try to feel the grief and understand Hamlet's mental breakdown brought about by the surrounding circumstances.

By working your way through the play several times, each time playing the part of a different character and trying to see their point of view, it will give you a better insight and help prepare you for the sort of questions you're likely to receive at exam time. Once you have formed your own interpretation, compare this with others', either in group discussion or by further reading.

If your mind works very visually, imagine key scenes

being performed. Who would you cast as Hamlet? Which actor would best convey Hamlet's character traits?

Always try to think about the writer – in this case William Shakespeare. What was he trying to achieve in a particular scene? Why did he decide to have a particular character say a particular line using a particular choice of words? Do certain words conjure up associations in your mind that he wanted you to notice? What do these associated ideas, or connotations, add to the presentation of the character or situation?

SUMMARY
- Before committing literary material to memory, get to know the text thoroughly by:

  1   taking an active role during reading
  2   developing empathy with one or more of the characters
  3   studying the interaction between characters.

- To help identify the main plot and theme, imagine it all taking place in a familiar geographical setting, and use people you know to act as the characters portrayed.

- Seek help from English literature guides, a dictionary of literary terms, critical essays and group discussions

- Learn some of the background of the author and the circumstances under which the text was written.

- To memorise a section of a play, a poem or a prose text, choose a familiar walk or journey to lay down individual lines which will preserve the natural order of the text.

- Use your imagination to translate key words or themes from a line into key mnemonic symbols.

- Then anchor these symbolic images along the various stages of your mental journey.

- Use association and the link method to understand and remember the meanings of certain words or phrases that have either changed or are obsolete now.

- You can reduce individual quotations into complex images and store them all in a familiar building, such as your local library or bookshop.

- Above all, use the combination of association and location with your inventive imagination to lift the text from its two-dimensional linear form, and bring the words alive by animating the characters and making the scenery vivid.

11 The Easy Route to Learning Languages

"I said it in Hebrew – I said it in Dutch –
I said it in German and Greek;
But I wholly forgot (and it vexes me much)
That English is what you speak!"
— Lewis Carroll (1832–98)

THAT SINKING FEELING

When I was taught languages at school I was told, for example, that the French for "floor" is *plancher* and it is a masculine noun. When I asked my teacher how I was supposed to remember this, he said the best way was to keep repeating the word until it eventually "sank" in.

As there was no apparent connection between the words *plancher* and floor, and no logical reason why on earth a floor should be masculine when a window was feminine, it seemed to me that this was the only possible answer my teacher could have given me. In other words, learning a language was going to be one long, hard slog.

ously having to repeat the same words over and
only to suffer the humiliation and frustration of
hem during vocab tests, was not my idea of fun.
....ue wonder I hated languages. Looking back, I compare the way I progressed to someone driving a car through
thick fog at night – in reverse gear and blindfolded! I knew
where I should end up but had no idea how to get there.

If only I had known about the method I am about to
describe, I am convinced that I would have achieved top
grades in Spanish, French and Latin and gone on to become
a competent linguist. Instead, I had to abandon Latin and
despite the effort put in, only gained minimal passes in the
other two. This is a great pity and I wince when I think back
on all the time I needlessly wasted.

The average amount of study time devoted to mastering
a foreign vocabulary can and should be severely cut, freeing
up more time for understanding the structure of the language, appreciating the culture from which it arose and
refining accent. If you follow the steps I am about to outline, it's possible to learn a basic vocabulary of 1,000 words
in ten hours, including the correct gender of the nouns.

If ever a subject were tailor-made for the methods I pre-
scribe, it's languages because full advantage can be taken of
the three main ingredients essential for memory development that you have already put into practice throughout
this book – association, imagination and location.

There are basically two ways to remember that "floor" in
French is *plancher*:

1   If there's no really obvious or memorable connection between a word and its foreign translation, then you need to create an artificial association. So imagine a floor made out of planks of wood with its previously unintelligible, coded, foreign equivalent. When you see the word *plancher* in future you'll immediately think: *plancher* – planks – wood – floor, and vice versa.

2   Monotonously repeat floor/*plancher* 200 times and hope for the best.

The briefest of extra time invested in the first method, by building a memorable stepping stone, will save all the soul-destroying repetition that the second method demands.

To remember that the German for rain is *Regen*, imagine hundreds of Ronald Reagans pouring from the sky. Now, I don't claim to be the inventor of a system that finds a link between a word and its foreign translation; indeed, there is a whole range of *Linkword* language books, each containing hundreds of ready-made mnemonic examples. Compiled by memory expert Dr Michael Gruneberg, they have proved to be of enormous benefit to anyone wanting to take a quick crash course in learning a new language.

However, what I will put my name to is a highly efficient system both for storing all these hundreds if not thousands of crazy images and for being able to instantly determine the gender of any given word. This is especially important if you are studying more than one language, because without a properly organised mental filing system, mass confusion can creep in. Trousers are feminine in German – (*die Hosen*) – and masculine in French (*le pantalon*). So how do you avoid mixing the genders up alongside remembering the words themselves?

TOWN PLANNING

Simple. You do so by incorporating the third crucial ingredient for memory training, the use of a familiar location. It's all very well creating bizarre, outrageous images, but it's essential to "place" them somewhere in order to have easy access to them at a later date. It's like opening all your wedding presents without making a note of who sent them. If you don't know where they came from, how are you going to know who to thank?

Whatever language you are studying, choose a familiar city, town or village to mentally store all the key images that you are going to generate, which will form your basic vocabulary. Think of the sort of words that you are going to learn: library, shopkeeper, vegetables, post office, traffic lights, wall, and so on. The layout of a village alone can accommodate an entire foreign vocabulary. Pick an area that you know well, as you are going to be weaving your way in and out of supermarkets, cafés, houses and car parks, and even climbing up trees. Then divide your town into sections. The local gardens, park or beauty spot could contain every conceivable adjective – wet, tall, strange, green, natural – and you could use the area in and around your local sports centre to group all the action verbs – run, lift, swim, hit, dive. But the real beauty of this system is that it allows you to separate words neatly into their respective genders by literally housing and containing them in what I call gender zones.

Women only!

Let's take French, for example. If your town or village is, say, split down the middle by a main road or high street, then all masculine nouns could be placed anywhere to the east of the street and feminine nouns to the west. The road acts as an effective, although somewhat antisocial, barrier or cut-off point preventing the two genders from ever crossing each other's paths.

By fixing your mind on a certain telephone kiosk in the eastern zone, you'll always remember that this word is masculine in French: *le téléphone*. Making a feature of a particular bank west of the high street will ensure your memory of its feminine status, *la banque*. There is no confusion, no extra mnemonic image involved. The geography of the location has magically lifted the burden of ever having to worry about gender again, as the very whereabouts of a noun automatically indicates its classification. You could almost call it cheating, as the town is acting as a pictorial reference. In fact, I would go so far as to say that you're not memorising genders at all. It is your imagination and a gender zone that are doing all the work for you.

If it's easier, you could use two or more cities to segregate the genders; German, after all, has three – masculine, feminine and neuter. As the cities of Bradford and Leeds are so close together, they would make ideal locations. Assuming you know the area, Bradford could be filled with feminine nouns and Leeds, to the east, would be an all-male zone. This leaves the area that lies between the two cities for all neuter words, the eunuchoid zone!

I recently taught this method to a student, Dave, who had been struggling with German. I was horrified that he couldn't even tell the difference between *der*, *die* and *das* (German for "the"), which are masculine, feminine and neuter, respectively. Considering that he had been studying the language for two years, that doesn't say much for the way he was taught. However, by getting him to use a little imagination and leaving aside, for the moment, correct pronunciation, this is how he quickly remembered the three different forms:

1 *Der* made him think of a dopey male pupil at school.
2 *Die* he associated with the word death and the funeral of his aunt.
3 *Das* made him think of a well-known soap powder that neutralises odours.

Dave had been advised to drop German and concentrate on other subjects, as his teachers felt he would almost certainly fail his final examination. In fact Dave managed to achieve a C grade, which was seen as a triumph by his parents and a mystery by his teachers.

Populating your town

To start building a basic French vocabulary, think of the layout of your own town or village and split it into two separate sections. As I take you through the following examples, use imagination and association to allocate suitable places in which to house the key images as they are formed.

- *La route – the road*

1   Wherever possible, use the correct pronunciation, in this case "root", to find a link between the French word and its English meaning. An obvious key image would be the root of a plant.
2   As *la route* is feminine you'll need to go to the female part of town. Picture a road that you are familiar with here, and then imagine a huge root sprouting out of the middle of it.

By the way, if you don't know the difference between *le* and *la* you should do! If not, think of Len and Laura.

- *Le chou – the cabbage*

1   As *chou* is pronounced "shoo", use a shoe as your key image.
2   This time, though, *le chou* is masculine, so choose a place in the males-only part of town where you are likely to find a cabbage. What about the market? Imagine the rather unsavoury sight, at one of the stalls, of cabbages growing out of old shoes.

- *Le marché – the market*

1 *Marché* is pronounced "marshay". I immediately think of a march.
2 As the word is masculine, imagine a big march taking place at the market you used in the last example. There are so many people that the cabbages get trampled on.

As you start to populate your town, linking key images of the same gender in this way all helps to reinforce and anchor the images to their locations.

- *La glace – the ice*

1 *Glace* sounds like "glass".
2 It's feminine, so hop back over to female territory. Someone has sculpted the shape of a glass out of the massive block of ice that has formed in your local fountain (assuming it's in the female gender zone, of course). Incidentally, both sculpture (*la sculpture*) and fountain (*la fontaine*) are feminine nouns.

Occasionally, you won't need a link word, as the French word will read the same as the English, but you'll still want to know the correct gender. In this case tag a symbolic image, like the French flag or a champagne bottle, to your key image in the appropriate gender zone of your town:

- *Le garage – the garage*

Picture a French flag outside a garage in your male sector.

How to park your adjectives

You could integrate adjectives into the gender zones, but I'm a stickler for keeping groups within their own confines. If they're all contained in the same area, you won't have so far to search when you're looking for an appropriate descriptive word. The following adjectives could all be accommodated in your local park.

Again, the same principle of finding a link word applies as before. This time, though, use your own creative ideas to provide key images for the background scenery:

English	key linking image	French
ugly	_____	*laid*
short	_____	*court*
quick	_____	*rapide*
angry	_____	*fâché*
pink	_____	*rose*
thin	_____	*mince*

Your park could well end up like a music festival full of ugly, **laid**-back hippies and short, **court**ly eco-warriors, which is then invaded by quick-talking **rap**pers, angry **fas**cists, pink **rose**s and thin strands of **mince**!

Where to find all the action

Action verbs, and indeed all verbs, could be stored at the sports centre or at your local health club. Keeping all the verbs under one roof at a specific location helps to avoid

137

confusion between them. Again, look for a suitable key image to link the French word and its translation:

- *Courir – to run*

Imagine a **courier** running through the entrance of the sports club to deliver something urgent.

- *Lever – to lift*

In the exercise room, there is a body-builder lifting a heavy **lever** which he or she uses as a makeshift weight.

- *Lutter – to wrestle, to struggle*

Picture a professional wrestler inside a wrestling ring struggling with a vicious **lute**. Listen to the twanging sound that the strings make. If your sports centre doesn't have a wrestling or boxing ring, create an imaginary one somewhere in the building.

- *Manger – to eat*

In the cafeteria, the members are being quite uncouth, eating out of a **manger**. Fresh **mang**o is the special dessert of the day.

- *Cacher – to hide*

Hidden inside one of the lockers you discover a huge quantity of **cash** that someone has tried to conceal. (Bear in mind that, in English, a cache is a hiding place for treasure, drugs or ammunition.)

- *Gérer – to manage*

The manager's name at the health club is **Ger**ry, only he's not that healthy, sitting in his office quaffing sherry all day.

The French for manager is *le directeur*. In this case, you would imagine someone you know who is a manager **direct**ing the traffic in the male gender zone, or if of the opposite sex, *la directrice*, in the feminine zone.

I always found it easier to translate from French to English, when I was at school, rather than from English to French, but using a key image enables you to translate in either direction because it works literally like a link, a stepping stone, a halfway point between one side and the other. Assuming you have been employing your imagination to visualise the examples throughout this chapter rather than just reading the words passively, you should have no difficulty in translating the following English words into French and vice versa, including the definite article (*la* or *le*) of the correct gender where necessary:

English	French
the ice	_____ ?
angry	_____ ?
the garage	_____ ?
the market	_____ ?
to hide	_____ ?
the cabbage	_____ ?

139

thin	_____	?
to run	_____	?
the road	_____	?

French	English	
rapide	_____	?
manger	_____	?
court	_____	?
lever	_____	?
gérer	_____	?
rose	_____	?
lutter	_____	?
laid	_____	?
la directrice	_____	?

Score 1 for each of the 18 translations, plus another 5 for the correct genders. You should have scored 23.

Anything less than 100 per cent means that you didn't make the necessary mental connections in the first place. Every word in that exercise – English or French – should have transported you off to a certain part of town where the key image would have revealed the translation. *Rose* takes you to the park where you can see the pink roses, and who's running into the sports centre? The courier, of course. The ice makes you think of the glass sculpted out of the frozen water in the fountain, which is located where? In the feminine zone (*la glace* – the ice). If you don't make the vital link to begin with, how can you expect to recall the words later?

More useful words for building your town

Feminine

la librairie	the bookshop
la pâtisserie	the cake shop
la boulangerie	the bread shop
la poste	the post office
la gare routière	the bus station
la cathédrale	the cathedral
une église	a church
la mairie	the town hall
la pharmacie	the chemist
la boucherie	the butchers
la station-service	the petrol station
la bibliothèque	the library
la banlieue	the suburbs

Masculine

le parking	the car park
le supermarché	the supermarket
le stade	the stadium
un hôpital	a hospital
le musée	the museum
le centre commercial	the shopping centre
le commissariat	the police station
le centre-ville	the town centre
le terrain de sport	the sports ground
le cinéma	the cinema

141

un hôtel	a hotel
le camping	the campsite
le quartier	the district

Days of the week

There's no limit to the amount and type of information your town can hold. If you're having trouble remembering the days of the week for any language, then apply the link method (chapter six) by making up a short story that links one day to the next. Use a suitable backdrop on which to anchor the scene, like the bus station. That's always full of timetables. And remember to be as creative as possible with the story. Here are the French days of the week:

Sunday	*dimanche*
Monday	*lundi*
Tuesday	*mardi*
Wednesday	*mercredi*
Thursday	*jeudi*
Friday	*vendredi*
Saturday	*samedi*

Don't worry about pronunciation; the images are acting purely as a reminder to trigger the correct word.

You can invent your own story, or here's one possible scenario: imagine you're at the bus station when you notice a **demon** is eating **lun**ch. He throws a **Mars** Bar at a passing **Mer**cedes. The driver, **Judy**, swerves into a **vend**ing machine ... quick, **Samedi** call an ambulance!

Numbers

If you have learnt the DOMINIC System (chapter nine), it won't take you long to associate the characters you selected to represent numbers with their French counterparts. For example, Albert Einstein represents the number 15; the French for 15 is *quinze*, pronounced roughly like "cans" in English. Fix an image in your brain, then, of Einstein standing by his blackboard giving a lecture while eating cans of baked beans. See if you can think of some images to go with some of your other DOMINIC System personalities, to enter the following French numbers in your memory bank:

1	un(e)	16	seize
2	deux	17	dix-sept
3	trois	18	dix-huit
4	quatre	19	dix-neuf
5	cinq	20	vingt
6	six	30	trente
7	sept	40	quarante
8	huit	50	cinquante
9	neuf	60	soixante
10	dix	70	soixante-dix
11	onze	80	quatre-vingts
12	douze	90	quatre-vingt-dix
13	treize	99	quatre-vingt-dix-neuf
14	quatorze	100	cent
15	quinze	1,000	mille

"Won't my head explode?"

In learning a language this way, some people are worried that their heads might fill up with too many mental images – that their thoughts might in some way get "crowded out" by an overwhelming population of bizarre scenes. These fears and criticisms are usually levelled, not surprisingly, by those who have never tried a method like this for themselves. If they did, they would soon realise that, ironically, the exact opposite of what they fear holds true – this method actually clears the mind by ordering data neatly.

It is interesting to note what the great Roman orator and statesman, Cicero, when discussing the art of memory, has to say on this very issue:

> "Nor is it true as unskilled people assert [quod ab inertibus dicitur] that memory is crushed beneath a weight of images and even what might have been retained by nature unassisted is obscured: for I have myself met eminent people with almost divine powers of memory, Charmadas at Athens and Metrodorus of Scepsis in Asia, who is said to be still living, each of whom used to say that he wrote down what he wanted to remember in certain **places** in his possession by means of **images**, just as if he were inscribing letters on wax. It follows that this practice cannot be used to draw out the memory if no memory has been given by nature, but it can undoubtedly summon it to come forth if it is in hiding."

– Cicero, *De Oratore* (emphases are mine)

Your memory will not be crushed beneath a weight of images because the method operates like a filing system. By converting a piece of data into a coded image and then storing it in a specific mental location, you are effectively filing it away. This means that you no longer have to worry about it because you are safe in the knowledge that it has a "place" of its own that you have access to and can refer to whenever you require it. In short, once the information is memorised you can forget about it.

Conversely, if information isn't processed properly and filed away neatly, then it hangs around in a sort of limbo, always showing its face and demanding your attention like an untidy desk piled high with unfinished business. If you want to clutter up your mind unnecessarily, try to cram a load of vocabulary by rote the night before an exam. The last thing you need as you walk into the examination room is a head full of words that you are desperately trying to remember by repeating over and over again.

If you install the mental filing system explained in this chapter, the only thoughts you'll be having before your exam are those of success.

Remember ...

The more you practise, the clearer your images will become. The clearer your images, the quicker you'll be able to generate them.

Paradoxically, the more images you create, the greater the capacity you'll have for storing them because your memory will rapidly become stronger, sharper and thirstier for more knowledge as it activates your mind and encourages a state of accelerated learning.

So don't give up after your first effort. If you're not used to using your imagination in this way, your brain is bound to feel a bit sluggish to begin with, just as your body does when it takes on a new sport. But persist and experiment because the rewards are too great to miss.

SUMMARY

- For each language, choose a familiar city, town or village to house all the words of a basic vocabulary.

- Organise your town to accommodate different types of words by dividing it into distinct sectors or ghettos. Create separate gender zones for masculine, feminine and neuter words, choose the sports centre for action verbs, select the local park for adjectives, and so on.

- By using imagination and association, create a link between the foreign word and its English meaning and turn it into a mental image.

- Once you have formed your key image, file it away by mentally "placing" it in a suitable area of town. This will then act as a pictorial reference guiding you to and reminding you of either the English word or its foreign translation along with the correct gender.

- Continue to build your mental filing system by adding

more key images as you spread them geographically throughout the town.

- One of the many advantages is the self-revising nature of this system. As the population of images increases in your town, so too do your memories of them. Each time you return or revisit your town you will be reminded of scenes and characters from the past. Vocabulary revision will begin to seem enjoyably nostalgic as you mentally saunter through your internal mnemonic world.

- I never thought I'd hear myself saying it but, armed with this technique, I wish I were back at school now!

12 Mathematical Short-cuts

"Multiplication is vexation,
Division is as bad;
The Rule of three doth puzzle me
And Practice drives me mad."
— anonymous Elizabethan manuscript (1570)

MENTAL ARITHMETIC

I can remember my days at junior school all too well. In those days, fear was thought to be the most effective tool for getting a child to remember his or her multiplication tables. As a penance for giving the incorrect answer to 9 × 7, I can recall being forced by my maths teacher to stand in front of the rest of the class and recite my "nine times" table. To make the humiliation even worse, each word I nervously uttered was accompanied by a light but positive whack to the backs of my legs with a ruler, just to drive home the message. "Nine ... whack, times one ... thwack, is nine ... whack ..." and so on.

The teaching of mathematics has changed significantly since my day, thankfully, with more emphasis on problem-solving, practical investigations and methods of doing calculations. The idea is to try to break down the perception of maths as a purely abstract subject by making it more interesting and enjoyable.

MATHEMATICAL DEFINITIONS

Maths has its jargon and specialised terminology just like any other subject. It is easy to think up simple ways to remind yourself of what the terms are and what they mean. Here are a few examples:

- *Equilateral triangle*

This is a triangle with all sides and angles equal. Look out for **equal** and **all** in the word **equil**ateral to remind you.

- *Scalene triangle*

All sides and angles different. Look out for s**ides** **all** **n**ot **e**qual in the word s**calene**.

- *Isosceles triangle*

Two sides and two angles equal. **1** **s**ide **o**dd – **iso**sceles.

- *Acute angle*

Less than 90 degrees. To remember that this is the smaller of the angles, think of **a cute** little kitten.

- *Obtuse angle*

Between 90 and 180 degrees. Think of a right-angle **o**nly **b**igger, **ob**tuse.

- *Sine, cosine, tangent*

Here's an old favourite for remembering the trigonometric ratios (the ratios between the lengths of the sides of a right-angled triangle):

Sine x = **O**pposite ÷ **H**ypotenuse
Cosine x = **A**djacent ÷ **H**ypotenuse
Tangent x = **O**pposite ÷ **A**djacent

Sir **O**liver's **H**orse **C**ame **A**mbling **H**ome **T**o **O**liver's **A**unt.

- *The mode*

This is the value which occurs most frequently in a set of data. Of the following set of numbers, 6, 2, 7, 3, 7, 3, 3, 2, 5, the number 3 occurs most often. So the mode of this distribution is 3. Think of **m**ost **o**ften **d**igit to help you remember this term.

- *Product*

The product of numbers is the result of multiplying them together. This is often confused with the word "sum", which is the addition of numbers. Think of **produc**ing offspring and the biblical phrase, "Go forth and **multiply**!"

- *Quotient*

The quotient of numbers is the result of dividing one number by another. Imagine receiving your **quota** or share of an inheritance that has been **divided** up among your family.

- *Order of operations*

The order of operations for complex mathematical equations is:

1 **Brackets**
2 **Multiplication/Division**
3 **Addition/Subtraction**

Just remember the handy mnemonic: **B**earded **M**en **D**ream **A**bout **S**having.

- *Rational and irrational numbers*

Rational numbers are ones which can be expressed as a fraction or a **ratio**: for example, $^1/_2$, $^3/_4$, 0.8, $^{17}/_2$. Irrational numbers cannot be expressed as either a fraction or a ratio: for example, $\pi = 3.1415926 \ldots$ π (pi) has been found to have millions of decimal places, with no end in sight. To remember this I think of memory expert Philip Bond, who memorised the first 10,000 decimal places of pi; you may feel that this is a rather **irrational** activity.

A MATHEMATICAL PARTY TRICK

In one of my television demonstrations, I am able to add up ten four-digit numbers blindfolded. Here's how I do it, and if you have learnt the DOMINIC System you'll be able to manage it too.

The first step is to prepare a location with just four stages, because you are going to generate four pairs of digits. Each pair of digits will be represented by a person using the DOMINIC System.

Picture the outside of your house. Looking at it face on, make the top left of the roof the first stage. Then down diagonally to the right you are going to have someone leaning out of the window. Just below this and slightly to the right will be a third person, standing on some ladders. Finally, at ground level and just to the right again will be your last character. The four people you end up with will form a rough diagonal line from left to right.

Now you are ready for the addition. With blindfold in place, ask someone to write down ten single-digit numbers in a column whilst calling them out slowly at the same time. As you hear the numbers add them up, and when you arrive at the total, translate it into a person. Once you have fixed the first person in your head and in position on your house, ask your helper to move on to the second column of digits.

For example:

$$
\begin{array}{r}
7\,3\,6\,4 \\
4\,2\,0\,1 \\
3\,8\,7\,1 \\
6\,7\,2\,8 \\
2\,6\,0\,9 \\
8\,7\,3\,5 \\
1\,3\,1\,2 \\
5\,2\,3\,6 \\
9\,0\,4\,3 \\
+\ 7\,4\,9\,2 \\
\hline
\end{array}
$$

Total of first column: 5 2 = EB   Enid Blyton
Total of second column: 4 2   = DB   David Bowie
Total of third column: 3 5 = CE   Clint Eastwood
Total of fourth column: 4 1 = DA   David Attenborough

In this example, 52 is the sum of the first column of digits. By converting this number into letters we arrive at the initials of Enid Blyton (EB = 52). Now, project the image of Enid Blyton on to the roof of your house. The bizarre sight of Enid and the Famous Five on your roof will remain as a powerful reminder of the number 52, which means that you are ready for the next column.

Working through the columns from left to right, repeat the process of adding up the digits in your head as they are called out until you arrive at the second total, 42, which is represented by David Bowie (DB = 42) positioned at the window. Again, by exaggerating the scene, this will secure your memory of the number.

The totals for the last two columns are 35 and 41, which give you Clint Eastwood (CE = 35) standing on the ladder and David Attenborough (DA = 41) supporting it from below at ground level. Now the entire sum has been reduced to just four simple images, which you can easily retain in your memory.

With all four players lodged firmly as a picture in your mind, you can now announce to your audience that you are going to add up the numbers in your head. As you prepare by reminding yourself of the images, tell your audience that you are quickly scanning through all the numbers, just to add to their bewilderment.

$$
\begin{array}{r}
5\,2 \\
4\,2 \\
3\,5 \\
+\quad 4\,1 \\
\hline
5\,6,5\,9\,1
\end{array}
$$

The key images are now perfectly positioned in your mind, allowing you to start slowly calling out the total from left to right as you carry out the last simple additions in your head for the tens of thousands column, the thousands column, the hundreds column and so on. Anyone watching will think that either you've got a photographic memory or you are a walking computer!

Whether you perform it as a party piece or not, creating sub-totals is an efficient and safe method of addition, as it reduces the chances of errors being made when carrying remainders in your head.

Try to get into the habit of rounding up or down certain numbers before adding them. For example, take the sum

$$59 + 85 = 144$$

This is much easier to calculate if you round 59 up to the number 60 first and then subtract one afterwards:

$$60 + 85 = 145 - 1 = 144.$$

Practise rounding up/down with the following sums and bid goodbye once and for all to your mental arithmetic headaches:

$$99 + 76 = ?$$

$$68 + 52 = ?$$

$$81 + 55 = ?$$

$$198 + 66 = ?$$

$$151 + 75 = ?$$

13 The Abstract World of Science

"Science is nothing but trained and organized common sense ..."
— Thomas Huxley (1825–95)

RETENTION AND UNDERSTANDING

How much of what we are taught in class do we think we retain? How much do our teachers think we understand?

There is increasing evidence, sadly, that not only do we retain very little, but we understand even less. According to a widely respected report by researchers at King's College, London, "the apparently acceptable level of examination performances hides disturbingly widespread areas of gross and damaging confusion".

Video interviews carried out by the Science Media Group in the USA have revealed that the message imparted by teachers during lessons, especially in the sciences, is being misinterpreted, partly owing to our own preconceived ideas about the universe.

At Saugus High School, Massachusetts, students were asked the following question before being taught about electricity: can you light a bulb using only a battery and some wire? They not only gave the correct answer – yes – but some of them also made reasonable drawings of a circuit diagram. However, after the teacher's presentation it was revealed that not only did the students' understanding of the phenomenon lessen, but they also became confused.

Typically, one student, Jennifer, produced a perfect circuit diagram – the sort that would command full marks in an examination. However, after the lesson, Jennifer didn't believe that battery and wire alone were sufficient to light a bulb. Why not? During the class, light bulbs had been displayed held upright in sockets. Her teacher Jim, with twenty-seven years of experience, assumed it was obvious that they were only there for convenience. But Jennifer developed a misconception during the lesson: she now thought that you can't light a bulb without a socket.

This revelation was to come as quite a shock to Jim and many other teachers who agreed to take part in these experiments. He said, "I thought I had got this thing down to the point where any dolt could understand what I'm doing ... the kids appear to be engaged, they sit there and nod sagely as if they're getting all of this stuff ... but it seems that they didn't really understand, grasp and internalise the concept that you thought you had presented to them in a clear way."

In our quest to understand science, we instinctively use common sense to produce personal interpretations of the world around us. The irony is that common sense can often mislead. Take the example of the man who is standing in a flat field with two bullets, one in a gun, the other in his hand. He shoots the one bullet straight ahead at exactly the same time as he drops the other.

- *Question: Which bullet hits the ground first?*

Answer: They both hit the ground at the same time. This may go against our intuitions, but in this case our intuitions are wrong – the forward momentum of the shot bullet doesn't matter because the downward force acting on both bullets (gravity) is the same.

SO WHAT IS THE SOLUTION?

How are we to control our wayward misconceptions and begin to grasp the rudiments of science?

- *Approach*

Well, of course, we'll always continue to apply common sense, but at the same time we should be ready to accept that things won't always turn out the way we expect them to. The world according to science is not always perceivable in the ordinary sense, so we must try to keep an open mind and build on our understanding of scientific principles – bearing in mind that as scientific study becomes more advanced, basic principles may be overturned.

159

- *Debate*

Rather than simply accepting answers, we should first discuss with others our individual theories on a certain problem. What happens when salt is added to water? Does it melt or does it simply disappear? By thinking, analysing and sharing ideas, we are automatically drawn inside a problem, with all the misconceptions laid out in the open for debate – and even ridicule – instead of being left to fester in unconvinced, suspicious minds.

The moment we realise that salt doesn't melt in water is when science begins. In fact, salt dissolves in water – the bonds holding the crystals of salt together come apart and the salt ions disperse through the water.

- *Question your teacher*

If it doesn't add up, say something. "Where's the logic?" "Please explain, I don't understand." Others will be grateful and so will your tutors – they need the feedback. Remember what Jim said, "They sit there and nod sagely as if they're getting all of this stuff." Who's kidding whom?

- *Be selective*

Inevitably, there is always more material in the curriculum than there is time available to learn it all, which means that there is often a rush to try to cover all the material. This can sometimes result in some topics being treated in less depth than others. The danger is that by trying to learn too much, our understanding is left behind. Whatever the pressure, try to specialise in certain fields. The mastering of just one or two key areas will boost your confidence and create a thirst for more knowledge in another field – the inevitable spin-off will be an improvement in your exam performance.

- *Add perspective*

Try to explore the wider world of science. The history, stories, anecdotes, chance discoveries and eccentricities of the great scientists do more than add a bit of colour; they also provide the background details and therefore the associations that are essential for anchoring our understanding of what often seems an abstract, incomprehensible soup of facts and figures.

HOW TO REMEMBER SCIENTIFIC TERMS

In science subjects like chemistry, physics and biology you will need to spend some of your revision time before an exam making sure that you can use all the terminology you have learned during your course correctly. The trouble is that most of the terminology you will have come across may not be intrinsically memorable. With a little mental inventiveness, however, you'll soon be able to understand the language of chemistry, biology or physics. You'll always find a connection somewhere if you look for it.

It is easy to create highly memorable images in your mind for just about any technical terms you might encounter. Take a little time (it doesn't take long) to make yourself a list of memory aids for the key terms you will need in the exam. To get you in the mood, here are a few chemistry examples:

- *Elements*

Elements contain only one type of atom. They cannot be chemically broken down into simpler substances. Think of Sherlock Holmes' famous exclamation, "**Element**ary, my dear Watson" – that is, nothing could be simpler.

- *Compounds*

These are substances which contain more than one type of atom, chemically joined. Compounds can be chemically split into simpler substances. Think of an animal **compound** containing several species.

- *Acids*

Acids are substances which:

1. turn blue litmus paper red: imagine a police officer and the "boys in blue" **turning red** with anger
2. have a sour taste: think of the taste of vinegar (ethanoic acid)
3. react with metals to form salts: visualise members of a heavy **metal** rock band at an acid house party turning into pillars of **salt**
4. neutralise bases: the **bass** guitar is **neutralised**.

- *Alloys*

Alloys are mixtures of metals formed by melting together two or more different metals and allowing the mixture to solidify. Brass, for example, is made up of copper and zinc. Think of **allies** joined together to form a solid front.

- *Deliquescence*

This is when a substance absorbs water from the air and dissolves in it to form a solution. To remind you, imagine walking into your local **delicatessen** and seeing a lemon sorbet that has been left out in the air too long and is turning into a runny liquid.

- *Efflorescence*

This is when a crystalline substance turns to fine powder on exposure to air, or when salts come to the surface of a substance and crystallise. Imagine an **effluent** containing dissolved detergent crystals drying out in the air, and the crystals turning into a powder.

- *Alcohols*

Alcohols are compounds of carbon, hydrogen and oxygen. You'll always remember this if you think of alcohol as "causing **h**ang-**o**vers". Ethanol, C_2H_5OH, is the alcohol found in drinks and produced by the fermentation of sugars from yeast.

- *Ions*

Ions are particles that carry an electrical charge, which might be positive or negative. Think of an electric **iron**.

- *Anions*

These are ions that have a negative charge. Imagine somebody called **Ann iron**ing a piece of **negative** film.

- *Cations*

These are ions that carry a positive charge. Think of cations as **pussy-tive**.

- *Exothermic reactions*

These are reactions that produce energy in the form of heat. Think of energy or heat **exiting**.

- *Endothermic reactions*

Reactions in which energy, as heat, is absorbed. Think of heat **en**tering.

- *Allotrope*

An allotrope is one of a number of forms that one element can take. Carbon, for example, has several markedly different allotropic forms, including graphite and diamond. Think of making different shapes or forms out of the same piece of rope – **a lot** of **rope** tricks. This is a good example of how to create very individual associations when faced with a term or phrase that has no obvious connection with its own meaning or definition.

- *Ammonia*

Ammonia is produced by mixing the two gases hydrogen and atmospheric nitrogen together in a ratio of 3:1 by volume. Using the DOMINIC System, imagine the three members of Charlie's Angels (CA = 31) squeezing the two gases together into one. The gas is manufactured by the Haber process, and then converted into ammonium compounds for making fertilisers, nitric acid, explosives and cleaning products, as well as some plastics. To remember all this, imagine going down to the harbour and seeing all these things as a shipment being lifted off a cargo boat. Ammunition will remind you of explosives, fireworks and night tricks, bleach is used in household cleaning, and the smell of fertiliser, like that of ammonia itself, is pungent.

You can see how easy it is to invent ridiculous images that will remain memorable in an exam so that instead of breaking your flow of thought by agonising over a definition you'll be able to recall the information easily and get on with your answer to the question. The same techniques can be applied to biological terms just as easily. Take the terms phenotype and genotype. It's easy to fix in your mind that **ph**enotype refers to the **ph**ysical signs of genotype – our **gen**etic composition. Physics, too, with all its complex equations, can be made visual and therefore memorable.

REMEMBERING PHYSICS EQUATIONS

Let's use as an example the ideal gas equation PV=nRT. This vital equation describes the behaviour of an "ideal" gas (P = pressure, V = volume, n = number of moles, R = the universal molar gas constant and T = temperature). First fix this in your mind with a mnemonic: how about **p**regnant **v**irgins **n**ever **r**eveal the **t**ruth. You can rearrange this to:

$$\frac{PV}{T} \quad \text{is constant.}$$

(pressure × volume ÷ temperature)

Think of someone **constantly press**ing a **volume** of gas over **hot** coals.

Remember that physics equations are not arbitrary – they describe real things. So you can often (although not always) use common sense to check them. Imagine a football full of air. When you squash it the pressure goes up as the volume goes down. Or think of heating up a gas in a rigid vessel (so V is fixed). The pressure increases until the vessel breaks.

Once you have committed to memory the equation

$$\frac{PV}{T} \quad \text{is constant}$$

then you already know two other expressions of the ideal gas law:

- *Boyle's Law: PV is constant at constant T*

Think of water **boil**ing at a constant temperature.

- *Charles' Law:* $\dfrac{V}{T}$ *is constant for fixed P*

Think of Prince **Charles** under constant media pressure.

These memory exercises can be taken even further. Returning to the world of chemistry, if you wanted to, it would be perfectly possible to use the link method and the DOMINIC System to learn the entire periodic table of elements off by heart – not that you'll need to for a chemistry exam, but if you really wanted to show off …

HOW TO MEMORISE THE PERIODIC TABLE

Some years ago I received a call from a television researcher asking if I would take part in a live "phone in" on daytime TV for students worried about taking their exams. Apart from offering tips, I was asked if I wouldn't mind, for demonstration purposes, quickly learning the periodic table on my way up to the studios.

When I'm asked to learn something like this in a hurry, I can only think that people must assume I have a photographic memory – a quick scan down the page and it's all lodged neatly in the brain. Unfortunately, I don't possess that ability and if I did I would probably be barred from entering any future memory competitions on the grounds of having an unfair advantage.

My brain is basically the same as anyone else's. The only reason why my memory works better than most is that I have learnt to feed information into my brain in such a way that I can guarantee retrieving it at a later date. What a pity I was never taught this learning technique when I was at school struggling with chemistry and all its elements.

Well, armed with a photocopy of the periodic table, I got on a plane at Heathrow and by the time I arrived at Liverpool, where the TV studio was located, I knew it back to front and inside out.

When I was eventually tested live on air, I was able to pinpoint precisely any of the 110 atomic numbers, symbols, groups and weights to four decimal places and it was assumed, wrongly of course, that I must have been referring to an exact mental photocopy of the table.

Although the techniques outlined in this book are basically simple to learn, trying to explain the mechanics of them in a few words is not an easy task, especially on television. If you start saying things like, "I imagine Horatio Nelson phoning Brian Epstein on top of an elephant" without adequate explanation, you run the risk of alienating your audience and being perceived as a complete nut.

Luckily, you know what I'm talking about, or at least you should do by now!

Elements and their symbols

It is important in the study of chemistry to know the symbols for the elements. Knowing the atomic number and which group each element belongs to is a sound basis for understanding the whole subject of chemistry. We usually learn which symbols refer to which elements by repetition and familiarisation over a period of time, in much the same way that we learn a language. In chapter eleven you discovered a short cut to learning a foreign vocabulary by finding a link between the foreign word and its English translation. The quickest way of learning chemical symbols is by using the same method.

For example, to remember that **Sn** is the symbol for **tin**, think of the cartoon hero **Tin Tin** with his faithful dog **Sn**owy. To connect **lead** to its chemical symbol **Pb**, try to imagine a **lead**-weighted **plumb**-line (the Latin word for lead is *plumbum*).

The symbol for **tungsten** is **W**, which comes from the name of one of the metal's ores: **Wolfram**. So picture a crazy mutant **Wolf** with **ten tongues** sticking out.

How would you link **gold** to its chemical symbol **Au**? What about: "I like the **au**ral ring of the word gold." Or: "The metal has a certain **au**ra about it."

Finally, **Hg** makes me think of the writer **H.G.** Wells; I think of **wells** of water contaminated with **mercury**.

The next time you have trouble remembering certain symbols, apply this method for an instant cure.

A memorable gathering

Looking at the way the first twenty elements of the periodic table are presented on page 177 is enough to put anyone off chemistry. Just imagine how daunting it would seem if you were asked to memorise all 110! Because the table is in list form, the information looks dull and uniform, and the groups or families to which each element belongs are camouflaged. It's like gazing at a guest list of twenty people invited to a party. One or two names might stick out, but trying to remember everybody would be difficult. However, once you've been to the party, chatted to individuals and seen everybody clumped together in various groups or cliques, you have a much clearer picture of that original list and plenty to gossip about, too – who was with whom and in which rooms. You remember it all (assuming you were reasonably sober) because you reviewed your experiences by playing back your mental video tape and associating each person with their surroundings.

So if you want to remember the first twenty elements, imagine them all gathered at one weird party! And once you've tried this, why not go on to do the whole 110?

Family planning

In chapter eight you memorised the alphabetical order of the twelve original European Union member states by taking a journey consisting of twelve stages.

To memorise the first section of the periodic table you will need to plan a location made up of eight rooms or areas. This is because the first twenty elements are divided into eight main groups or families:

Group no.	Group name
0	Noble gases
1	Alkali metals

2	Alkaline-earth metals
3	Boron group
4	Carbon group
5	Nitrogen group
6	Oxygen group
7	Halogens

The numbers 0 to 7 that I have assigned to the eight groups above correspond with those used in a conventional periodic table (they relate to the configuration of electrons in the elements).

I have left the element hydrogen out of this exercise -- it is easy to remember as it is the lightest element, with the atomic number 1.

Your school or college would make an ideal location for memorising the elements, as you can use the various classrooms, lecture theatres, labs, assembly rooms and recreation areas to house the groups. By designating and cordoning off specific areas for each group, you will avoid confusion between families. Your understanding and knowledge of the elements will be greatly enhanced because you will effectively bring them alive by creating an animated, three-dimensional representation of the periodic table. Give each room or area its own colour code as an extra mnemonic aid or memory back-up.

To remember the atomic number for each element, you are going to combine personalities from the DOMINIC System (I'll use my characters as examples – you should use your own) with imaginary objects triggered by the names of the elements to form complex images – the chemistry between them should be fascinating and memorable!

Let's begin with group 0, the noble gases:

helium

neon

argon

As we're making a start, we might as well use the chemistry lab as a place to store these gases. To remind you that they belong to **group 0**, picture a big **blue football** at the door of the lab. Football is a number shape for 0 and blue will be the colour code for this group.

As you enter the room the first thing you see is the film actor Orlando Bloom sitting in a blue **helium** balloon. This image will remind you that the atomic number of helium is **2**. Orlando Bloom (OB = **02**) from the DOMINIC System is used as the person, and the helium balloon provides the prop involved in the action.

02	*Helium*
Orlando Bloom	*sitting in helium balloon*
(person)	*(action)*

It's important to fuse your complex image to its surroundings. Have the balloon causing havoc by knocking equipment over all around the lab – test-tubes go flying as it bobs about. This will help to anchor your images and animating the scenes will make them much more memorable.

Next, you find Wild West star Annie Oakley (AO = **10**) kneeling **on** the floor. She is lit up by a bright blue **neon light** which makes her cowgirl outfit glow blue. This complex image makes it easy to remember that neon's atomic number is **10**.

If you work your way clockwise round the room you will preserve the ascending order of atomic numbers. Refer to the periodic table at the end of this chapter to cross-check how the element names and numbers are being linked together as we continue.

Moving on, you see Adolf Hitler (AH = **18**) doing a spot of **argon** welding, causing blue sparks to fly in all directions.

Here is a summary of those images:

Noble gases

Location = chemistry lab
Group = 0 (shape: football)
Colour code = blue

Element	Person (atomic no.)	Element prop
Helium	Orlando Bloom (02)	helium balloon
Neon	Annie Oakley (10)	neon lights
Argon	Adolf Hitler (18)	argon welding

Having formed your gaseous images, revise the data by taking a quick mental stroll around the lab. Don't be put off by the seemingly long-winded nature of this method. What may take several sentences for me to describe can be visualised by you in a split second, and by recapping the scenes in the lab just once, you'll find that they're pretty firmly fixed in your brain already.

Remember, too, that you should substitute your own people to represent the atomic numbers and use whatever action suggests itself to you to make a link between the person representing the atomic number and a memorable prop for the element's name.

Now that the noble gases are all firmly installed in the chemistry lab, think of a place for the alkali metals to gather. The college dining area perhaps?

Alkali metals

Location = dining room
Group = 1 (shape: candle)
Colour code = yellow

Element	Person (atomic no.)	Element prop
Lithium	Oliver Cromwell (03)	?
Sodium	Andre Agassi (11)	?
Potassium	Alfred Nobel (19)	?

Now it's your turn. Using the layout of your college dining hall, try to find a prop or association for each of the three alkali metal elements and an action to link it to each of the atomic number personalities from your own personal DOMINIC System list. This time, you see a tall yellow candle burning with a bright yellow flame at the entrance to the

THE ABSTRACT WORLD OF SCIENCE

dining hall. A candle is the number shape for 1 and yellow is the new colour code, which will permeate throughout each scene taking place in the room.

When looking for associations with elements, try to exploit their uses or characteristics. For example, lithium is used to help treat people suffering from manic-depression, so you could visualise a manic Oliver Cromwell, in full Civil War uniform, haranguing all those present as he waves a bright yellow musket around. Sodium, one of the elements in salt (sodium chloride), could be represented by Andre Agassi dancing round the room wearing a yellow T-shirt, and sprinkling salt on the floor as he goes.

When you've finished your scenes to fix each alkali metal element in the dining room, move on to the next groups:

Alkaline-earth metals   Location = locker rooms
                                      Group = 2 (shape: swan)

The boron group   Location = physics lab
                                      Group = 3 (shape: handcuffs)

The carbon group   Location = art room
                                      Group = 4 (shape: sailboat)

The nitrogen group   Location = biology lab
                                      Group = 5 (shape: curtain hook)

The oxygen group   Location = gymnasium
                                      Group = 6 (shape: mallet)

Halogens   Location = assembly hall

                        Group = 7 (shape: boomerang)

Continue to work your way through the various areas of your college, creating bizarre scenes as you go. Notice, too, that there are links, however tenuous, between the type of rooms and the group headings. Carbon is found in the art room, and you need plenty of oxygen in the gymnasium.

Can you see how all the pieces are joining together like one big jigsaw? Of course, there is nothing to stop you from deepening your knowledge of each element still further. All you have to do is expand the scenes by adding further detailed images. For example, if you really felt the need, you could include atomic weights. A crazed Bill Oddie (BO = 20) goose-stepping (action of Adolf Hitler; AH = 18) around the kneeling Annie Oakley and wearing handcuffs (number shape for three) will ensure you'll never forget that neon's atomic weight is 20.183.

Once you have fixed all the elements firmly in your mind by arranging them ingeniously throughout your mnemonic network, you will have gained a much clearer perspective of the vital first section of the table , and will also better appreciate the relationships between them. This will, I have no doubt, greatly facilitate your understanding of chemistry when you come to study the intricacies of molecular structures and chemical reactions.

And once you've memorised the first twenty elements in the periodic table (listed right), if you really want to impress, get yourself a copy of the complete table – all 110 elements – and let your imagination go wild!

THE FIRST TWENTY ELEMENTS

No.	Element	Symbol	Weight	Group
1	Hydrogen	H	1.00797	Hydrogen
2	Helium	He	4.0026	Noble gases
3	Lithium	Li	6.939	Alkali metals
4	Beryllium	Be	9.0122	Alkaline-earth metals
5	Boron	B	10.811	Boron group
6	Carbon	C	12.01115	Carbon group
7	Nitrogen	N	14.0067	Nitrogen group
8	Oxygen	O	15.9994	Oxygen group
9	Fluorine	F	18.9984	Halogens
10	Neon	Ne	20.183	Noble gases
11	Sodium	Na	22.9898	Alkali metals
12	Magnesium	Mg	24.312	Alkaline-earth metals
13	Aluminium	Al	26.9815	Boron group
14	Silicon	Si	28.086	Carbon group
15	Phosphorus	P	30.9738	Nitrogen group
16	Sulphur	S	32.064	Oxygen group
17	Chlorine	Cl	35.453	Halogens
18	Argon	Ar	39.948	Noble gases
19	Potassium	K	39.102	Alkali metals
20	Calcium	Ca	40.08	Alkaline-earth metals

14 How to Remember History Dates

"History is a cyclic poem written by time upon the memories of man."

— Percy Bysshe Shelley (1792–1822)

MASTERING YOUR SUBJECT

Traditionally, history has always been regarded by students as a hard slog. But if the right learning strategy were used, not only would students achieve higher grades by doing less work; they would also find their studying immensely absorbing. Mastering history requires three things:

1 Extensive reading
2 Analysis
3 Imagination

In exams, you are going to be tested on your knowledge of events, their related causes and their consequences. As well as a good knowledge of facts, you will be judged on the depth of your understanding and personal insight into these events. You will need to recreate the past by having an empathy with the major players and ordinary people of the time, getting inside their heads and really achieving an understanding of their beliefs, attitudes and culture and of how these would have shaped their actions. This requires an active imagination motivated by an enquiring, curious mind and a discerning eye for drawing information out of contemporary source material.

Learning history can be compared to constructing a huge jigsaw puzzle. By joining one or two pieces together, you may be able to pick out certain shapes and form various sections of the puzzle. But it's not until all the pieces that make up these sections are joined together that the true overall picture can be fully appreciated.

The pieces of the history puzzle can be gathered from many sources, such as articles, diaries, letters, books and wills. It helps if you enjoy reading, but even if you're not a bookworm a healthy interest can be developed by visiting museums, historical sites and seeing drama, films and videos. History at its best consists of a balance between gaining knowledge of key facts and developing investigative skills. It is honing your investigative abilities that will make the subject more rewarding and enjoyable.

The ideal way to learn about a historical event would be to travel back in time to the period in which it took place and experience it at first hand. As we clearly cannot do this, an alternative might be to reverse the process – to recreate history by bringing the events and all the characters involved in it alive now. To help you to piece together all the facts and understand the interactions between historical characters, you need to use a familiar location and people you already know to act as substitutes for the real ones.

RECALLING A HISTORICAL PROCESS

By supplying your imagination with people and places to act as links to key names, dates and events, it is really an incredibly simple task to fix important historical episodes firmly in your brain. Using this method will ensure that you have facts at your fingertips, filed chronologically and accurately, for deployment in exams to support the points you are making in your essays.

As an example, we'll use the Russian Revolution. The entire sequence of events could be mentally re-enacted in a nearby village. It doesn't matter where you live; you can always find places to associate with the past. Your local petrol station, for example, could be used to represent Petrograd, where the workers began to riot. The Winter Palace could be represented by a country house or hotel; Jack Nicholson could play the part of Tsar Nicholas II; John Lennon could be Lenin; your local butcher, perhaps, could stand in for Joseph Stalin, instigator of brutal purges.

Overleaf is a summary of key dates and events in the Russian Revolution:

1917

10 March:	Workers in Petrograd start to riot. Run out of flour, coal and wood. Freezing temperatures worsen situation. Inefficient bureaucracy. People fed up with costly war against Germany.
12 March:	Winter Palace falls when 1,500 loyal troops surrender.
16 March:	Tsar Nicholas II signs abdication papers on board the imperial train. Provisional government set up under Prince Georgy Lvov.
21 March:	Former Tsar and Tsarina arrested.
16 April:	Lenin returns to Russia from exile in Switzerland. He travels in a sealed train, courtesy of the Germans, who know he will cause difficulties in Russia.
17 April:	Lenin publishes his "April Theses", which demand transfer of power to workers' soviets.
16 June:	Soviet Congress opens and laughs at Lenin's announcement that Bolsheviks aim to rule Russia alone.

16 July: Bolshevik uprising in Petrograd. Half a million people on streets. Provisional Government suppresses uprising. Lenin escapes to Finland, dressed as a fireman.

22 July: Kerensky appointed Russian Prime Minister.

13 August: Kerensky tells King George V of Britain that Russians will continue to fight in war against Germans.

15 September: Kerensky declares Russia a republic.

17 September: Russian army routed at Riga by Germans. Riga is only 350 miles from Petrograd.

30 September: Tsar and family moved to Siberia by Kerensky to protect them from Bolsheviks.

20 October: Lenin returns to Petrograd.

23 October: Bolsheviks vote to start an armed uprising against Kerensky's Provisional Government. The beginning of the October Revolution.

7 November: Bolsheviks overthrow Provisional Government in a bloodless coup.

Armed squads of Bolsheviks take over railway stations, post offices, telephone exchanges and banks.

Bolsheviks occupy cruiser *Aurora*, which raises the red flag and anchors in the Neva opposite the Winter Palace.

Aurora fires blank shell. Red Guards storm the Winter Palace and its members are arrested.

Lenin heads Bolshevik regime. Leon Trotsky appointed as foreign minister.

Life in Petrograd largely undisturbed. Public transport continues, shops stay open.

1918

3 March: Bolsheviks sign humiliating peace treaty with Germans, the Treaty of Brest-Litovsk.

16 July: Tsar Nicholas II and family massacred by Red Guards in a cellar.

1919

4 March: Bolsheviks establish Comintern, abbreviation of Communist International, to encourage world revolution.

1924

21 January: Lenin dies.

1940

───────────────────────────────────

20 August: Trotsky killed with an ice-pick in Mexico
City.

All the events listed could easily be reconstructed in your
mind using a little imagination. To remember the dates,
you would combine your scenes of mental re-enactment
with the DOMINIC System for numbers. Most of the key
events took place in 1917. Imagine Alec Guinness as the
manager of your local petrol station, confronted by rioting
workers marching on his forecourt.

Alec Guinness (AG = 17) reminds you of the year, 1917.

Petrol station = Petrograd.

The workers **march**ing gives you the month, March. If
you wanted to remember the precise date, 10 March, you
could use Annie Oakley (AO = 10) as the leader of the
march, brandishing her guns.

Imagine icy conditions with snow falling as a reminder
of the freezing temperatures.

The garage shop, which is normally stocked up with
bread, coal and wood, is completely empty.

This is an extremely effective memory aid because by
transforming cold, faceless facts into colourful, animated
three-dimensional scenes, you are feeding the information
to your brain in a form that is much easier for the brain to
latch on to and interpret.

You could go on to recreate the scene of Tsar Nicholas II's

abdication in your head by imagining yourself on the same train, travelling along a familiar route. Visualise someone you know called Nicholas and watch him reluctantly signing the abdication form. Try to see as much detail as possible. Which station are you approaching? Feel the tension of the moment and note the expression on Nicholas's face. Again, if you wanted to remember the date, 16 March, why not have Arnold Schwarzenegger (AS = 16) as the ticket inspector marching down the carriage?

When it comes to trying to remember facts, figures, dates and awkward names, mnemonics can play quite a role in history. Take the name Kerensky, for example. Although Kerensky was a man, there's no reason why you shouldn't use a substitute such as Karen, someone you know, on a pair of skis. It doesn't matter how you arrive at the name, just as long as the method works.

During a corporate after-dinner speech, I may have to remember both the first names and surnames of as many as 150 people, and on occasion swot up on the personal history of individuals, their position in the company and even their birthdays. As these are people I have never met before, I have to use all kinds of outlandish, crazy and unspeakable associations to remember them by. So crazy, in fact, that I can't fail to remember them and so unspeakable that to reveal to certain individuals my associations would get me into serious trouble. So be inventive with your ideas, but keep them to yourself!

MASTERING HISTORICAL JARGON

In history you will also come across quite complex technical vocabulary. If you don't understand some of the words, don't just pass them by; get your dictionary out. Once you discover the meaning of a word or term, use a link or mental stepping stone to ensure that it stays firmly lodged in your memory. Here are some examples:

- *Oligarchy*

A small body of people who have the supreme power of a state in their hands – in other words, a government run by the few.

Think of the words '**of little**' to help you remember the word and its meaning.

- *Anarchism*

The teaching of anarchists – those whose ideal of a society is one without a government of any kind.

The prefix **an-** comes from the Greek, meaning without; and **arche** is Greek for rule. Once you know this you can unlock the meaning of several similar terms, such as matriarchy (rule by women) or patriarchy (rule by men).

- *Totalitarian*

Belonging to a form of government that controls everything under one authority, and allows no opposition.

Just think of **total** control.

187

- *Autocracy*

Similar to despotism, an absolute government by one person. An autocrat is one who rules by his own power.

Auto comes from the Greek, and means self. Think of words like **auto**biography or **auto**graph to remind you of the action of one person.

- *Legislature*

A law-making body. Having power to make laws.
   Think of the word **legal**.

- *Judiciary*

A body of judges; a system of courts.
   Easy to remember if you think of **judges**.

- *Reactionary*

One who attempts to revert to past political conditions.
   Think of someone you know who doesn't like change and is always **react**ing against it – Grandad, perhaps!

Developing vocabulary is important, and choosing the right word to back up your arguments will impress your examiners and show that you have a good understanding of your subject.

SOME MEMORABLE DATES

Lists of random dates can be tricky and tiresome to memorise. But by converting numbers into persons and actions and linking them to the events, it doesn't take long to lock such a list – such as the following one of important events in world history – firmly in one's memory bank.

1170	Thomas Becket murdered
1215	Magna Carta signed
1415	Battle of Agincourt
1455	Wars of the Roses
1492	Columbus sails for America
1642	Start of English Civil War
1666	Great Fire of London
1773	Boston Tea Party
1776	Declaration of Independence (US)
1789	Storming of the Bastille
1805	Battle of Trafalgar
1914	Start of World War I in Europe
1939	Start of World War II in Europe
1945	United Nations formed
1949	NATO formed
1956	Suez Crisis
1963	John F. Kennedy assassinated
1969	First man on the Moon

Here are a few examples to show how easily dates can be brought to life.

- *1170*

Saint Thomas Becket, after a long quarrel with Henry II, was murdered in Canterbury Cathedral. To remember the date and the associated event I would imagine Andre Agassi clubbing poor Becket to death with a golf club as he prays at the altar. The first two digits are the person, in this case Andre Agassi (AA = 11). The last two digits become the action. I always link the number 70 with golf (GO = 70).

- *1455*

The so-called Wars of the Roses were struggles between the Yorkists and Lancastrians for control of the throne and government. I would use the bizarre complex image of the Artful Dodger (AD = 14) running into battle with gladioli and a big red rose between his teeth. Here, gladioli are the attribute of Edna Everage (EE = 55). Remember, we only require an action for the last two digits, so Edna is nowhere to be seen, but her spirit lives on in the "gladys".

- *1773*

At the Boston Tea Party, 342 chests of tea were thrown into Boston harbour in protest against tea taxation.

I arrive at the unlikely image of Alec Guinness (AG = 17) wearing a stethoscope testing for heartbeats on men who have collapsed under the effort of throwing chests. The stethoscope belongs to George Clooney (GC = 73).

Experiment with your own complex images to remember the other dates. How, for example, would you link the English Civil War with 1642 using Arnold Schwarzenegger (AS = 16) and putting on make-up (the action of David Bowie (DB = 42)?

Using simple association, and the DOMINIC System to translate dates into people, it's possible to introduce a whole cast of interesting characters, and bring a difficult subject to life. Who said learning history was dull?

15   Geographical Tips

*"For one country is different from another; its
earth is different, as are its stones, wines,
bread, meat, and everything that grows and
thrives in a specific region."*
— Paracelsus (1493–1541)

A WORLD OF MEMORY

Geography is a good example of a subject that draws upon a broad range of cortical skills, including the spatial and analytical skills involved in drawing, reading and interpreting maps, graphs and diagrams. Memory plays a key role in this subject, as a knowledge of facts is essential. You'll need a good grasp of river systems, earthquakes, volcanoes, erosion, climate, weather systems, and soil, as well as an understanding of human geography, including population, town planning, transport and economic development.

With so much data to learn, it's got to be worthwhile investing in a system that can help you absorb it all swiftly and efficiently, so that you can get on with the task of understanding and applying it.

Your studies may include a comprehensive analysis of one particular country. The best way to build up such a dossier on a specific country is to prepare a separate and familiar location for it. All data relating to Germany, for example, could be stored in the form of key images at a friend's house, while statistics relating to the Netherlands might be kept in a shopping precinct. If you have visited the country in question and know a specific location there, use that as the basis of your mental file.

Once you have designated a "place" for each country, you can start filing away facts and statistics by converting numbers into key people using the DOMINIC System. Choose a key image for each type of information or statistic, such as popcorn to denote population.

To remember that the population of the Netherlands is 16 million, first transport yourself to the shopping mall and create an image of Arnold Schwarzenegger (AS = 16) handing out popcorn to crowds of fans.

The most famous image of Britain is Big Ben and the House of Commons, so why not use that area to store all the statistics on Britain? Imagine *Gone with the Wind* heroine Scarlett O'Hara (SO = 60), for example, clinging to the top of Big Ben while chewing on a bag of popcorn to store the fact that the population of Britain is 60 million.

The following population figures are easy to file away mentally once you have organised a site for each country:

Country	Population		Personality
Germany	82 million	HB	Humphrey Bogart
UK	60 million	SO	Scarlett O'Hara
France	61 million	SA	Salvador Allende
Australia	21 million	BA	Ben Affleck
Netherlands	16 million	AS	Arnold Schwarzenegger
Austria	8 million	OH	Oliver Hardy
South Africa	44 million	DD	Donald Duck

Use your own cast of personalities to represent the relevant numbers and don't forget to create really way-out images to fix the data firmly in your mind.

CAPITALS

You may need to remember capital cities to link data to them or to discuss differences in urban and rural conditions in different nations. The way to make sure you never forget the correct capital for a country is to approach the task in the same way as learning a foreign vocabulary. The trick is to find a link between the country and its capital by forming an exaggerated and memorable key image.

The city of Kiev, for example, is the capital of Ukraine. I associate Kiev with chicken, as in the garlicky dish chicken Kiev, and Ukraine makes me think of a tall mechanical crane. So my key image is of a huge, smelly chicken dangling from a tall crane. Take a look at the following list and form your own crazy, memorable links. Remember to use humour, exaggeration, movement, sexuality and colour.

Country	Capital
Switzerland	Berne
Belgium	Brussels
Afghanistan	Kabul
Nepal	Kathmandu
Romania	Bucharest
Philippines	Manila
North Korea	Pyongyang
South Korea	Seoul
New Zealand	Wellington
Grenada	St George's
Cuba	Havana
Dominica	Roseau
Turkey	Ankara
Uruguay	Montevideo
Chile	Santiago
Indonesia	Jakarta
Singapore	Singapore
USA	Washington, DC
Bulgaria	Sofia

Here are some suggestions, but your own creations will work best for you:

- *Switzerland – Berne*

Invent a new ritual for the Swiss. Imagine one of them standing on top of a mountain yodelling with one trouser leg rolled up exposing a **bare** knee.

- *Afghanistan – Kabul*

Imagine that all **cabs** in Afghanistan are driven by **Afghan** hounds. This should act sufficiently as a trigger, but you can always add a **bull** to the back of the cab to reinforce the link.

- *North/South Korea – Pyongyang/Seoul*

I'm sure Koreans both north and south of the border would be unimpressed by my associations, but this is how I avoid confusion between their capitals. I imagine walking into my local **careers** centre and noticing a dreadful **pong** hanging in the air, detected by my **no**se (north). The smell is coming from a **south**erly direction … the **soles** of my feet!

- *New Zealand – Wellington*

You should try to use the countries themselves as a backdrop for your key images. However, if you have no pictorial association with a particular country, use its shape from a map. For example, if you look at the shape of **New Zealand**, it's like a **Wellington** boot held upside down.

- *Grenada – St George's*

Picture the legend of **St George** and the dragon, only this time he is using a hand **grenade** to slay the beast.

- *The United States*

The method works just as well for remembering individual

American states and their capitals. Imagine being told to tarmac the vast, flat terrain of **Salt Lake City** in Utah – in other words, **you tar** (Utah) Salt Lake City. Or perhaps the singer **Lulu** has suddenly been bestowed with a great **honour** in **Hawaii** – Honolulu being that state's capital.

MEMORISING LISTS OF DATA

To store a list of information in order, such as the largest oceans or deserts, the longest rivers, highest mountains, and so on, use either the journey method or the link method. Here are the world's largest oceans and seas:

1   Pacific Ocean
2   Atlantic Ocean
3   Indian Ocean
4   Arctic Ocean
5   Arabian Sea
6   South China Sea
7   Caribbean Sea
8   Mediterranean Sea
9   Bering Sea
10 Bay of Bengal

To remember the order, I would form a short journey along a familiar coastal route divided into ten stages. Next, I would reduce the name of each ocean or sea to a key image. My father would represent the Pacific (Pa), an atlas the Atlantic, an Apache for Indian, and an iceberg would remind me of the Arctic Ocean. Lastly, I would anchor each key image at various stages along my coastal route, secure in the knowledge that the journey will preserve the correct order. Have a go with the rest of the list.

Statistics involving area, height, length and depth of the oceans and seas could all be accommodated by adding more images to the relevant locations. The masses of data to learn in geography are more than matched by the abundance of mental geography in which to store it. You will be able to memorise key data connected with whatever topic you are studying: development statistics, tectonic plate names, examples of climate variables, migration figures or demographic data such as countries' GDPs, energy consumption figures or life expectancy.

16   A Brain for Business

"Here's the rule for bargains: 'do other men
for they would do you.' That's the true
business precept."
— Jonas Chuzzlewit in *Martin Chuzzlewit*
by Charles Dickens (1812–1870)

THE LANGUAGE OF BUSINESS

If there is one area of modern life that employs enough jargon to make your brain burst, it is the world of business. This jargon – the specialised language and terminology used to describe the systems and concepts central to the business world – cannot be avoided in business studies exams. It's just got to be learned.

The trouble is, the language of business is forever changing as the media invent phrases to sum up new trends or practices. One of these is the term "white knight" – which I recall being used when the classic British china company Wedgwood was saved from a takeover by the London

Rubber Company (the famous condom manufacturer) by another company. This second company arrived like a "knight in shining armour" with a counter-offer for Wedgwood, and saved the blushes of ladies sipping from their Wedgwood china at many a refined tea party.

Different companies may use use commonly understood business terms in their own ways, and you'll often find that they use different terminology for the same thing. For instance, some companies talk about contribution costing while others talk about marginal costing; both are referring to the same financial strategy.

WHAT DOES IT MEAN?

Of course, there is no point committing either of those terms to memory without also providing yourself with a prompt as to their meaning. Anyone can scatter jargon liberally through their exam answers, but the key to success is proving that you can use it appropriately and with secure understanding.

Thankfully, many business terms are invented to reflect established or emerging practices in a colourful and memorable way, often using images and associations. Well known examples are bull markets and bear markets. It's easy to work out which is which: a **bull market** is a period when stock market prices are rising and enthusiastic speculators charge in like **raging bulls**, mad to buy up shares in the expectation of huge profits; a **bear market** is the opposite – a time of pessimism and falling prices when everyone wants to sell shares so that they can buy them back later at a lower price. I always think of a grumpy "**bear with a sore head**".

Not all business jargon is quite so visual, of course, but there is usually a clear logical link between a term and its meaning. Let's go back to the financial terms "contribution costing" and "marginal costing". Put simply, **contribution costing** is the value of a product based only on its variable cost, so only taking into account the **contribution** it makes to the overheads of the business; **marginal costing** is the same, because it reflects the contribution the product makes to the business's profit **margin**. When committing these concepts to memory, you are still using associations – verbal instead of visual ones in this case – to fix term and meaning firmly together in your brain.

TIME TO TALK TERMS
Here are some suggestions for how to memorise terms from a key area of business: marketing. Have a go at applying the same principle of association to any of the terminology you will need for your exam.

- *Boston matrix*

This is a method of analysing the position of a company's products in terms of their market share, growth and how they support each other's development. It is a sophisticated system of analysis, which really is the **boss**'s **mat**e in terms of planning. To remember how this particular product portfolio system differs from others, focus on this idea of

203

one product being the **mate** of another, that is helping it to grow or change. The four categories of product included in the matrix are:

- *Dog*

This is a product with low market share in a market with low growth. Think of a really scruffy, old dog that's definitely on its way out.

- *Cash cow*

This is a product that has a high share of a declining market. The Boston matrix shows how a firm can use the cash generated from these brands to invest in newer products with greater potential for growth. Think of a rather thin and mangy cow that has banknotes stuck all over it.

- *Problem child*

This is a product with low market share in a rising market. Think of a moody child with a lot of growth ahead of it, but a real attitude problem.

- *Rising star*

This is a product with high market share in a rising market. Think of a shooting star soaring up into the night sky.

To remind yourself of the entire matrix, visualise the weird scene all together: the **boss** looks out of his or her window at a sick **dog** limping away as a bewildered looking **cow** tries to chew on all the banknotes stuck to itself, while a moody **child** snatches some of the money, the rest of which forms the glowing tail of a shooting **star**.

Now try applying the same techniques of association and imagination to the following marketing terms:

- *Predatory pricing*

The practice of setting a price low enough to drive competitors out of the market or even out of business.

- *Consumer durable*

A household product which is expected to last for three years or more.

- *Above the line promotion*

The advertising of a product through the media.

- *Below the line promotion*

The promotion of a product through sponsorship, competitions or special offers.

17 Mind over Media

"Where the press is free and every man able to read, all is safe."

— Thomas Jefferson (1743–1826)

THINKING FOR YOURSELF

These days, our world is absolutely saturated in electronic and print media. These technological means of communication – television, radio, film, the press, advertising and the internet – tend to be one-way traffic. We sit and consume them. Switch off our critical faculties and absorb all they throw at us. Not great, you might think, for stretching our mental capacities.

In fact, it is exactly this characteristic that makes the subject of media studies so interesting.

In media studies you learn to develop what's known as critical autonomy – in other words, thinking for yourself.

To do this, there are a number of important concepts that you need to master – key theories, debates, research findings and ideas relating to the media. You can't succeed in this subject without deploying these concepts effectively during exams. And the tool you need to use to ensure that you have the conceptual armoury you need, ready and primed for use? Your memory.

REFLECTION OR REPRESENTATION?

The first thing to realise about the media is that it does not offer straightforward reflections of reality. What it actually provides are artificially created representations of reality. And these representations are created in their own characteristic forms and languages. In addition to learning how to recognise these forms, you will also need to commit to memory the jargon needed to write critically about them.

MEMORISING THE CRITICAL CONCEPTS

Making abstract concepts memorable takes the addition of just one key ingredient: imagination. Take, for example, these key terms vital in analysing media texts:

* *Semiotics*

This simply means the study of signs and symbols, so to remember how to talk about the semiotics of a media text – the symbols in it that represent certain ideas – think about the commonly used symbol of the **tick**, in this case, a **semi-hot** one.

- *Genre*

This is a type or style of media text. Think of the **general** rules for each type of film or feature under discussion.

- *Denotative meaning*

This is the straightforward, superficial meaning of a media text, so think of someone just **noting down** the text exactly.

- *Connotative meaning*

This is the implied meaning: the one that is not obvious, but is created by associations in our minds. Think of the media institution that has created the text **conning** the audience or consumer into having a certain reaction.

Sets of critical concepts often surround one particular area of the media or of your study of the media. In an exam, you need to make sure you don't leave a crucial critical idea out of your analysis. For this, imaginative mnemonic words or phrases, constructed out of the first letters or syllables of the key ideas, are invaluable. If the ideas should be applied in a particular sequence or form the stages of a process, the order of your mnemonic phrase will be vital. Otherwise, just play around with the order of the words you need to remember until they suggest a memorable phrase. Bear in mind that for case of memorisation, the sillier, more outrageous or personal the word or phrase you come up with, the better. Using rhyme or other sound effects works well

209

too, and keeping mnemonic phrases short and punchy is vital. Here are some examples to get you thinking:

- *Media audiences*

Some of the key concepts to keep in mind when writing about audiences, whether of electronic or print media, are audience **positioning**, **target** audience, **scheduling** considerations, audience **power**, size and **constituency** of the audience, and **segmentation** of the audience by the media.

Position tar in **shed** for **power con**-**sent**.

- *Documentaries*

Key concepts in analysing documentary techniques are selection of material, how editing has been used, the effect of the narrator, the set-ups used and the entertainment function of the documentary. Think of the overall **sense** of the documentary.

The functions of documentaries could be social, informative, educative, political, illuminative or empathetic. Think about your diet: "should **I** eat **pie**".

- *Newspapers*

To remember that a critique of press coverage may need to include considerations such as the dangers of inaccuracy and **fabrication**, issues of **privacy**, use of **sensationalism**, creation of **propaganda** and an emphasis on **personalities** rather than news, remember that a **fab private sense** creates a **prop**er **person**.

You can see how easy it is to create ridiculous but memorable words and phrases, so that when you get into your media studies exam you can feel confident that you will quickly be able to bring to bear whatever key concepts are relevant to the question you are asked. And thinking about these media debates and issues is not only useful for exams. In our information society, knowledge of the workings of the media and an ability to think critically is increasingly valued in the workplace.

18   ICT with Imagination

"Language is a part of our organism and
no less complicated than it."
— Ludwig Wittgenstein (1889–1951)

A VIRTUAL LANGUAGE

For me, what distinguishes the related fields of computing and of information and communication technology (ICT) from other areas of study is their extreme and sometimes quite baffling use of abbreviations and acronyms. Listening to an ICT expert explain a computer problem to me is often like trying to take in the random lists of letters sometimes used for memory challenges. While most of us know what RAM and ROM stand for (random access memory and read-only memory, in case you didn't) and some of us could even work out what an ISP is (internet service provider, in case you were wondering), when it comes to

LANs, WANs, URLs and WIMPs, I personally start to get seriously lost. To succeed in these subjects, however, you've got to become fluent in the "virtual" language that describes the workings of this virtual world.

EXPANDING YOUR CAST OF CHARACTERS

To do this, you can draw on a range of the memory techniques you have learned in this book, all of them relying on imagination and association: number–shapes, the "people" of the DOMINIC System (see pages 98–106), and the creation of scenarios for your "people".

Use the number–shapes that you devised on page 96 to represent the ten letters used in the DOMINIC System (see page 99) when standing on their own. For pairs of letters, refer to the DOMINIC System itself, which gives you a host of ready-made personalities queuing up to represent one hundred two-letter combinations (see pages 102–105) in your imagined scenes. You then have the potential to conjure up one thousand three-letter combinations.

If an acronym has letters that are not included in the DOMINIC System, I use the NATO Phonetic Alphabet, or international radiotelephony spelling alphabet, which was invented in the 1950s to make spellings intelligible to NATO's allies. These words are well known and widely used, and memorable images can be formed from them.

The complete NATO alphabet is given opposite, for your reference. The ten letters that are already included in the DOMINIC System are shown in italic type.

A	Alpha	N	November
B	Bravo	O	Oscar
C	Charlie	P	Papa
D	Delta	Q	Quebec
E	Echo	R	Romeo
F	Foxtrot	S	Sierra
G	Golf	T	Tango
H	Hotel	U	Uniform
I	India	V	Victor
J	Juliet	W	Whisky
K	Kilo	X	X-ray
L	Lima	Y	Yankee
M	Mike	Z	Zulu

Of course, you may prefer to create your own imaginative associations for the letters not in the DOMINIC System – friends' or relatives' initials, names of places that are important to you, standard country abbreviations, names of bands or organisations. Include whatever will be the most memorable for you so that you can form an unchanging reference list that will always be at your disposal.

By using a combination of all these methods, you will find that any number of ICT-related acronyms and abbreviations can be made memorable, and can be linked both to their simple meaning and to their practical application.

LOOKING AT LETTERS

Here are some examples of abbreviated ICT terms made memorable by combinations of the techniques that have just been explained – acronyms have never been so visual:

- *ADC*

The Artful Dodger (AD), wearing handcuffs (number shape for 3; 3 = C) is busy changing variable quantities of air into digits. The handcuffs are hampering his efforts and the scene is chaotic as digits fly out of his hands while he does his best to be a human **a**nalogue-to-**d**igital **c**onverter.

- *DAC*

Naturalist David Attenborough (DA), similarly handcuffed (number shape for 3; 3 = C), struggles to change the digits back to their natural state, as a **d**igital-to-**a**nalogue converter.

- *BACS*

Ben Affleck (BA) is robotically paying Claudia Schiffer (CS) her wages in a human version of a **b**ankers' **a**utomated **c**learing **s**ervice.

- *CAD*

Charlie's Angels (CA) are clustered around a computer terminal, busy designing a flag (number shape for 4; 4 = D) in their own stylish effort at **c**omputer-**a**ided **d**esign.

- *URL*

A uniformed (U) Romeo (R) is working as a tour guide in the Peruvian capital, Lima (L), pointing out tourist facilities all over the city as a **u**niversal **r**esource **l**ocator.

- *LAN*

Also wandering around the Peruvian capital, Lima (L), scientist Alfred Nobel (AN) has found a new and unlikely job knotting fishing nets in order to make the city's residents a **l**ocal **a**rea **n**etwork.

- *WAN*

Finding inspiration in a glass of whisky (W), Alfred Nobel (AN) manages to really knuckle down and work on his net to enlarge it into a **w**ide **a**rea **n**etwork.

- *WIMP*

This one's easy – think of the weakest, wimpiest person you know and imagine them pointing feebly at a window with an icon of Mickey Mouse on it, making them a **w**indows **i**con **m**ouse **p**ointer.

There are a great many more ICT and computing acronyms like this. They can all inspire memorable images into which you can incorporate not only the words themselves but also imaginative triggers to help you remember the definitions of the terms.

19   Giving a Presentation

*"There is no such thing on earth as an
uninteresting subject; the only thing that
can exist is an uninterested person."*
— G. K. Chesterton (1874–1936)

PRESENTING YOURSELF

More and more, students are required to give short presentations either to their fellow pupils or to their lecturer. Occasionally they may be one of a team of presenters, each making his or her own specialised contribution to an overall subject for discussion.

For may of us, speaking in public can be a daunting, if not harrowing, experience. Our fears usually centre on the following issues:

- *Vulnerability*

Many students hate the thought of being the focus of attention or being "put on the spot" lest, by saying the wrong things, they lay themselves open to criticism and ridicule.

- *Memory loss*

The nightmare scenario is a long, pregnant silence as you fall into a chasm of amnesia, exacerbated by the intense, quizzical glare of your expectant audience.

- *Fear of failure*

Any images of failure you harbour in the lead-up to the presentation can give rise to stress, stage fright, nervousness and anxiety, worsening any lack of confidence.

Take comfort, at least, from the fact that all the best speakers have at some point shared these fears and anxieties. Multimillionaire film director Steven Spielberg says that, next to insects, his greatest fear is speaking in public. Once, during a conference he was giving to students of American law, he suddenly forgot how to speak English, his mother tongue! So he tried to think in French. The experience, which lasted a minute or two, was, he says, terrifying. The panic that gripped him literally rendered him speechless.

There is no such thing as a natural speaker. So-called "natural speakers" only appear so because they have worked hard at their trade and have learnt from their mistakes over a period of time. If you are inexperienced at speaking, just remember that not only will the audience be on your side, but they too will have to give presentations; so they will be sharing the same anxieties and will appreciate the difficulties that you're up against.

In the words of Franklin D. Roosevelt, "the only thing we have to fear is fear itself". The aim of this chapter is not only to help you deliver a speech entirely from memory, but also to help dispel any of those fears of the unknown and replace them with confidence-building, positive thoughts. Giving a speech can and should, believe it or not, be an enjoyable, fulfilling experience.

PLANNING YOUR PRESENTATION

One of the best ways to prepare your presentation is by first drawing out all your ideas in the form of a Mind Map, as described in detail in chapter three. Get all your thoughts out in the open initially by chucking them down on a single sheet of paper. Identify the core idea of your speech and place it in the centre of the paper in the form of a symbolic image. If I were planning a speech on memory, for example, my central image would be an elephant. I would then allow a quick release of associated thoughts and ideas to flood out and emanate from this image without worrying about priority, sequence or sentence structure at this stage. The branches would include "mnemonics", "number systems", "demonstrations", "history of", and so on.

By laying out a speech in this fashion you are providing yourself with an effective overview of the subject, which helps you to clearly identify the key areas and points that are worthy of discussion.

Apart from your own thoughts, ideas and knowledge on the topic, more information can be added to your Mind Map from other sources, such as books, interviews or videos. It's important to gather as much information as you can before imposing an order on your presentation. If you commit yourself to a specific order straight away, you run the danger of continually backtracking, which will prolong the planning of your speech unnecessarily and may result in an imbalance of contents.

Let's suppose you are part of a small group of four students, each of whom is giving a talk on the success of women in art. You have chosen artist Angelica Kauffmann as the subject of your speech, which you are expected to deliver as interestingly and effectively as possible.

The following is a brief account of the artist's life. As a useful exercise, prepare a short talk from this by creating your own Mind Map. Lift the salient facts from the text and place them as key words and symbols along the various branches that spread out from the central image.

Angelica Kauffmann

Angelica Kauffmann was born to a Catholic family in Switzerland in 1741. She was a prolific artist eagerly sought after for her portrait-painting by a large international clientele. Her father, Johann Joseph Kauffmann, a painter in his own right, was a great source of encouragement and taught her the basic techniques of drawing and painting. A precocious child, she became an accomplished artist by the age of thirteen and showed skills in music too, then a more normal pursuit for young women.

After her mother died, Kauffmann turned professional at the age of sixteen and travelled with her father to Florence, an important centre for the study of painting and sculpture. One of her many successes was, at the age of twenty, to be made a member of the Academy of Design in Florence – a rare achievement for a woman in those days.

In 1763 she moved to Italy, where the ruins of ancient Rome provided a bountiful source of architectural and sculptural models, which she studied keenly. Although she became very famous in Italy, she did not find much work in the form of commissions from Italians and they did not pay very well. She was, however, popular with British visitors, which influenced her decision to move to London in 1766. Her fluent English soon helped her to establish herself through many of her aristocratic contacts. Two years later she was one of only two women to become a founder member of the Royal Academy of Art. She also helped to establish a school of history painting in England.

Kauffmann's success was accelerated and assured by her large portrait of the Duchess of Brunswick, which was very well received. She wrote to her father saying how excited she was about the subsequent visit by the Princess of Wales (the Duchess's mother) to her studio, an honour that no other artist had ever received.

Sir Joshua Reynolds became a close friend of hers and helped to establish her reputation. In the eighteenth

223

women were usually restricted to still-life painting
e not allowed to attend life classes at the Royal
ᵣ that involved nude male models. However,
nn's time in Italy had already equipped her with a
wide knowledge of ancient sculpture and understanding of
human anatomy. This was to influence her paintings,
which portrayed mythological gods and goddesses. Her
style can be described as Neoclassical, with portraits of
female sitters among her finest works.

Kauffmann became one of the most successful women
artists, both critically and financially, in the history of art –
an exceptional achievement for a woman living in the
eighteenth century.

She retired to Rome in the 1780s with her husband
Antonio Zucchi, and died there in 1807.

When you have completed your Mind Map, compare it
with mine (on page 34) to see if there are any similarities.
Although the written account contains some 450 words,
most of the information on the Map can be read and
understood at a glance. The written representation, besides
being rather repetitive and looking unappetising and somewhat intimidating, leaves you with no feel for the relative
importance of the facts of Kauffmann's life. The Mind Map,
on the other hand, has made the whole thing more palatable by providing you with an instant overview, showing
you that there really wasn't that much to take in and learn
after all. Notice, too, how all the facts have been efficiently

sorted and connected to four main branches or groups, allowing you to reel off the various biographical details without having to search through numerous lines of text.

Organising the running order

Once you have collated all the information and can "see" the extent of your speech, you are ready to apply some form of order to it. All you have to do is to number the key words as you run through the speech in your head. I suggest you pencil in the numbers initially in case you decide to change the running order or add more information later on.

You may wish to kick off your presentation by saying, "Angelica Kauffmann was one of the most important women in the history of art. Her most notable successes were … She was born in Switzerland in 1741 …". You would remember this opener by putting the number 1 next to the branch word "success", and the number 2 by the key word "born", and so on. The Map can be used as a sort of script for the entire speech, with the key words providing mental triggers and the numbers guiding you through the order of your points.

Remember that a good speech has a beginning, middle and end. The Mind Map will provide the body of the presentation, but it's worthwhile spending time to prepare separately a colourful introduction and conclusion. Afterwards it's usual to invite questions from the audience.

Try practising your speech by talking to an imaginary audience and, if you can bear to, make a recording of your own voice so that you can judge the delivery for yourself. The more you become accustomed to the sound of your own voice over several dummy runs, the easier and smoother it will be on the day.

Don't try to memorise your speech word for word – you'll alienate your audience or even send them off to sleep. It is the spontaneity of your own thoughts and interpretations that people want to hear, and the key words will keep you on track.

Look, no notes!

Being a memory man, I am expected to give talks entirely from memory without the luxury of even a Mind Map. But achieving this is a lot easier than people think. If you are at the stage where all your key points are numbered, you are only one step away from total recall. All you do is translate the key points of your speech into associative key images and place these at various stages along a familiar route, using the journey method.

In chapter ten, I showed you how to memorise a Shakespeare soliloquy by reducing each line to one or more key images, and then depositing them at significant stages along a favourite walk or at various points on a golf course. The principle for memorising a presentation works in the same way, except, if anything, it's a lot easier: you won't have the added pressure of having to remember your lines word for word. You are, after all, supposed to be giving a account, not somebody else's.

If you find the prospect of having to give a presentation a bit depressing, cheer yourself up by choosing a location which you associate with happy memories as your back-drop – a favourite holiday spot, such as a seaside resort, for instance. Once you have decided on a suitable location, start weaving your way mentally around the various houses, restaurants, beach huts, and cliff tops, counting off a number of stops along the way. The number of stages on your journey will depend on the number of key points you require to deliver the whole speech. This can vary according to the type of material and amount of detail contained in your speech, as well as your knowledge of the subject matter. To give you an idea, I would normally require a route consisting of about fifty stages to deliver a one-hour talk.

Now let's run through the first few lines of the account of Angelica Kauffmann using a holiday location in Rock, north Cornwall. Remember, these are my images and my associations, and they took very little time to generate, as will your own. For me to describe the images in words and ask you to visualise what I'm expressing takes a little longer, so don't be put off by what appears to be a long-winded process. In fact, the method is quite quick.

After briefly introducing myself and the subject of my talk, this is how I would remember the facts in order:

- *Stage I:*
  Angelica Kauffmann was born to a Catholic family in Switzerland in 1741.

The first stage of my journey is the grave of the late English poet Sir John Betjeman. I said you should choose a place that evokes happy memories, and this one does for me. This is a beautiful spot overlooking the Atlantic and set in the grounds of an old church with a characteristic bent spire.

My key complex image is of David Attenborough carrying a baby with a rosary round its neck. Behind, I can see tall, snowcapped mountain peaks.

The baby indicates Kauffmann's birth. David Attenborough (DA = 41) gives me the year 1741. The rosary symbolises Catholicism. The snowy mountains I associate with Switzerland.

- *Stage 2:*
  She was a prolific artist eagerly sought for her portrait painting by a large international clientele.

The second stop on my route is at one of the clifftops at Rock. Here, I imagine a long line of people of mixed races eagerly queuing to have their portraits painted by an artist sitting next to a stack of spare canvases.

The complex image speaks for itself, except perhaps for the spare canvases: these are there to remind me of Kauffmann's highly productive, prolific nature.

- *Stage 3:*
  Her father, Johann Joseph Kauffmann, a painter in his own right, was a great source of encouragement and taught her the basic techniques of drawing and painting.

The third stage is down on the beach, where I see a friend of mine, Jojo, standing by a blackboard holding a paintbrush in one hand and a pencil in the other.

Jojo triggers the father's name and the blackboard is the symbol for teaching.

- *Stage 4:*
  A precocious child, she became an accomplished artist by the age of thirteen and showed skills in music too, then a more normal pursuit for young women.

My next stop is a beach bar known as the Last Resort. Inside I visualise American gangster Al Capone juggling a piano with a paintbox in front of an audience.

Al Capone (AC = 13) gives me Kauffmann's age. The piano reminds me of her musical skills. Juggling the piano with the paintbox provides me with a pointer to Kauffmann's precocious talent.

If you know your subject reasonably well, you won't need to use so many key images. If you were already familiar with the details of Kauffmann's early life, for example, then a single key image of a baby would be sufficient to remind you to talk about her childhood.

Once you have laid all the key points of the speech along your mental route, you can start practising your delivery with the aim of dispensing with notes. After a few trial runs, you should know the contents of your speech backwards and forwards.

ADVANTAGES

Memorising your presentation doesn't take long. It will not only fix the material in your head for possible future exam use, but it will also make your presentation go really well – for the following reasons:

- *Eye contact*

Have you noticed that when politicians speak from a podium these days they seem able to maintain unbroken eye contact with their audience? What is more, they are able to keep this up for long periods without the apparent use of any written notes.

This is not because politicians' memories are any better these days, but simply because they have an invisible autocue. This consists of two transparent sheets placed strategically in front of the speaker. Words, which the audience cannot see, are electronically produced on each sheet, one at a time. As a result the speaker's head does not move from left to right as he or she is reading the words, giving a false impression of direct eye contact – a classic way of capturing an audience's attention. When I give a talk from memory, the mental journey acts as my own invisible autocue. Only this one is the ultimate idiot board: it can't be detected by anyone. I appear to be looking directly into people's eyes as I read off images from my own mind's eye.

Eye contact is important because it:

1 puts you in closer contact with your audience

2 accentuates what you are saying

3 makes your audience feel involved

4 puts you in full control as you can see everything going on around you

5 will make what you have to say more convincing

6 leaves your audience thinking you know your subject well (even if you don't think so yourself!)

- *Smoother delivery*

The mental journey helps you deliver your words more smoothly because as you can see the key points ahead of you in the form of images, you will have time to prepare yourself for the next point.

The trick is to look at the key image at a stage, talk about its contents and, as you near the end of a sentence, move on in your mind to the next stage to get a quick sneak preview of what it holds in store. The result is that you'll always keep one step ahead, allowing yourself enough leeway to smooth over any gaps between key points.

In the unlikely event of your forgetting the actual key image at a particular stage, there are two alternatives. First, the fact that you can't remember it probably indicates that its contents aren't that critical to the speech anyway, in which case just skip to the next stage. Second, it's always comforting to have a backup. So keep a separate written list of the key points on a piece of paper – not that you'll ever need to refer to it on the day!

- *Confidence*

Knowing that you are able to stand up in front of a crowd of people and deliver a speech entirely from memory is a great confidence-booster. If you know the journey well and the images on it are easily recalled, there's no danger of your drying up or losing the running order. Without the fear of forgetting, there's no pressure; it's easy.

- *Now where was I?*

One big advantage of using this method is that if at any time you get distracted in some way, there's no danger of losing your place because you'll always remember, from your internal geography, where you left off. Often someone will ask me a question which will force me to deviate from the order of my presentation, or an unconnected idea may pop into my head that I may then expand on. When I've exhausted this particular unplanned avenue of thought, the journey will get me back on track because all I have to do is recall where I was last standing on my mental walk.

This is particularly useful if you're one of those people who, like me, has a runaway imagination or is easily side-tracked. It's like driving along a road and deciding to turn off because an interesting sight has caught your attention. It's easy enough to find your way back to the road once your curiosity has been satisfied. Your presentation is a journey with a starting point, stops along the way and a final destination. That is why this method works so well.

VISUAL AIDS

Whether you use flip charts, transparencies, slides or photographs, visual aids can greatly enhance a presentation. Because you are adding another dimension – sight as well as sound – it's not surprising that the right visual aid can increase one's memory of a speech by as much as 90 per cent. As well as adding wider cortical appeal by engaging your audience's right brains as well as their left, visual aids help to drive home your message by providing graphic or illustrative proof of what you're saying.

Moreover, if you find that the glare of "all eyes on you" is a little overwhelming, then a visual diversion will provide you with at least some temporary relief. It will also help to maintain the attention of your audience by adding colour and contrast, can save you a lot of time, and sometimes speaks more accurately than words ever can.

Finally, there's no reason why you shouldn't use visual aids as memory aids themselves. If you were talking about Angelica Kauffmann you would, no doubt, have acquired reproductions of her work. You could use objects appearing in her paintings as triggers for key points of discussion.

Next time you have to give a speech, try using a mental journey to memorise it. And if you apply the DOMINIC System you'll be able to rattle off facts, figures, dates and statistics, which will greatly impress your lecturers and fellow students.

20 Planning Your Revision

*"The mind is not a vessel to be filled but a fire
to be kindled."*

— Plutarch (46–127CE)

TIME AND NOTION

The first thing to do when it comes to revising is to make a plan. It is vitally important that you organise a timetable to ensure that all the subjects you need to revise receive adequate attention.

How much time will I need?

Quantify the amount of work required for each subject. You must have some idea of the size of the task in hand before you can divide up your revision time, as some subjects will require more attention than others. Study the syllabus for each subject so that you know exactly what you are supposed to have covered, and get hold of past exam papers. Most important of all, seek advice – if anyone knows what work is involved, your teacher will.

How much time have I got?

Once you have an estimate, measured in hours, of the total time required to complete your revision, work out how much time you can reasonably allocate to covering it, during both term time and holidays. Hopefully, you should end up with a surplus of spare time.

Now you are ready to draw up a timetable. Make sure you allow for breaks. The ideal arrangement is to have short bursts of twenty minutes of concentrated study, followed by five minutes of rest or a complete change of activity. In other words, for every two hours of study, allow for an extra half hour's break time. Studying in short bursts optimises your learning rate for several reasons.

- *The feel-fresh factor*

If you don't take regular breaks, your brain will gradually start to switch off through boredom, overload, lethargy or fatigue. It's like trying to read a long essay that has no full stops or commas. Your brain craves a bit of light and shade to maintain its interest and keep that feel-fresh factor.

- *Taking stock*

Strangely enough, despite the fact that your attention may suddenly switch to feeding the cat or filtering the coffee, your brain actually carries on working by taking stock of all the information that's just been fed to it. Although you may not be conscious of it, it continues to process, sort and save data, filing it away in your memory banks whilst you've got your feet up and are munching on a cream cake. So don't feel guilty or think that you're wasting valuable time by taking breaks; allow your mind some time to "get its breath back" – but not too long!

How often should I revise a topic?

If you have just been learning a new topic, the simple answer to when you should next review it is immediately; then 24 hours later, one week later, one month later, three months later and so on.

Let's assume that the subject is biology, and you have just been studying the human respiratory system. Today is 1 January. After a short break, revise by refreshing your memory of the main points.

Afterwards, write down your notes – in the form of Mind Maps or the layout of a familiar location – on the next review date: in this case, 2 January. The following day, go over those same points again, but this time your new review date will be 9 January. Now switch to a different subject and apply the same format, always adding a new review date at the end of each review session. Box off a section in the cor ner of your notes specifically for keeping dates.

It is very important to rotate subjects, for example by revising some biology, some geography, some maths and so on. That way you'll maintain your interest with an element of contrast, rather than stagnating and getting bogged down in one subject.

Keep to your plan!

Having devised your timetable, keep to it! We humans are creatures of habit, which means we all too easily fall into the habit of avoiding tasks by using delaying tactics and allowing distractions.

Creating a timetable is like making a pledge: once you've agreed to it, it cannot be broken. Regarding it in this way will help prevent procrastination because you will not allow yourself the alternative of, "Well, never mind, I can always catch up tomorrow."

Ritual

You can turn this otherwise negative side of your habitual nature into a positive advantage by developing a study ritual. If you plan to work from 7.30 p.m. till 10 p.m., for example, give yourself a countdown of activity starting, say, from 7 p.m. This could involve doing a crossword, playing computer games or engaging in some form of physical exercise. It doesn't really matter, as long as it becomes a routine preamble for studying.

I speak from experience. Having an active imagination, I am vulnerable to the lure of distraction and am not naturally disciplined in the art of "getting down to it". But I have found a very effective way of overcoming this problem.

IMAGINATION AND STRESS BANISHMENT

One of the reasons that we find it such an effort to settle down to work is that the mere idea of study can evoke in us so many negative feelings, emotions and associative images. A typical split-second flash of associations may follow a line of progression rather like this:

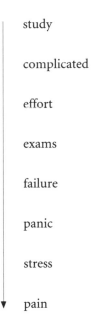

study

complicated

effort

exams

failure

panic

stress

pain

In short, study = pain, which is hardly an incentive to get started on a revision timetable

There is a reason for stress. Its function is to warn us of impending danger, and so it protects us by prodding us into taking counteractive measures.

Unfortunately, though, this incessant prodding can go too far and end up being counterproductive.

OK, so you realise that you should have started your revision much earlier; now you're prepared to do something about it. The trouble is that stress levels are high, and the images of the exam room and your relatives' disappointed faces loom ever nearer, which means you can't concentrate. This is unfair; you've accepted intellectually that there is an urgent need to act, but you're hampered by the physical and emotional effects of the stress triggered by your realisation.

Some may compare the following remedy with practices such as meditation, self-hypnosis or neurolinguistic programming. I prefer to call it "getting in the right frame of mind". It is a method that I cultivated independently, and it not only banishes stress, but allows me to tackle any form of study head-on.

1   Lie on your back or sit comfortably in an armchair.
2   With your eyes closed, focus your attention on every muscle in your body, starting with your feet. As you work your way up, let go of any tension in those muscles until your whole body feels like a heavy, dead weight. Feel the tension go in your face muscles and let your jaw sag as it succumbs to the gravity.
3   With the rest of your body taken care of, you can now concentrate on your breathing, heartbeat, and any feelings of nausea caused by the anxiety of stress.

4 Breathe deeply and slowly, even though your heart may be pumping furiously.

5 Now, using your imagination, try to translate whatever feelings of tension, pain and nausea you may have into an associative tangible image. For example, the occasional nauseated sensation I feel at the back of my throat I picture as a slow trickle of tiny, greyish pellets. Lower down in my chest they gather into a heaving mass of sticky, soot-covered ball bearings. Whatever your representation, imagine a hand gently dipping into your body, grabbing the offending objects and throwing them far away. Continue the process until most of the stress has been removed.

6 With your body relaxed, your breathing deep and your nausea reduced, conjure up an image of a place or person that gives you a peaceful, happy or relaxed feeling. This could be a scene from your childhood, a holiday location or a loved one. Latch on to that image, and try to immerse yourself in those pleasant feelings.

7 Now, slowly superimpose that pleasant picture on to the image of your anxiety. You might, for example, visualise walking into the examination room and seeing your loved one standing there. In my case, I use the scene of a quiet casino with a croupier standing at an empty blackjack table (that always gives me a good feeling!). But sitting on the table is not a pack of playing cards, but ... a word processor, which normally represents work, deadlines, accounts and other aspects of responsibility. By

241

blending or mixing the two images together – one of happiness, the other of anxiety – I am in effect neutralising the object of my fear.

8   Having stared my worst fears in the face and removed any bad feelings associated with them, I can now approach the job in hand in a completely relaxed, positive state of mind.

Try this method yourself. It certainly works for me, and it could help you too.

A Final Word

The path to success lies before you. It is not an exclusive path with access granted only to a privileged few who are born with a special gift for learning. It is available to everyone. You are already well equipped with an incredible potential for absorbing knowledge. Let your imagination – the key to learning and memory unleash that brainpower and propel you along at ever-increasing speeds.

The techniques, systems and methods I have revealed in this book are a product of experience. They are the result of a process of selection which has taken years of research to develop. The methods which failed have been discarded, and only the most effective and successful remain. Apply them and you will reap more than just success in exams; you will acquire an insatiable appetite for learning. Bon appetit!

Index

Bibliography

Apps, J.W. *Study Skills for Adults Returning to School*, McGraw-Hill (New York), 1982

Baker, S. *The Practical Stylist*, Harper & Row (New York), 1985

Brink-Budgen, R. van den *Critical Thinking for Students*, How To Books (Oxford, UK), 2000

Brookes, K. *Exam Skills*, Hodder Children's Books (London), 2002

Brookes, K. *Revision Sorted*, Hodder Children's Books (London), 2002

Brookes, K. *Top Websites for Homework*, Hodder Children's Books (London), 2002

Buzan, T. *Make the Most of Your Mind*, Pan (London), 1988

Buzan, T. *Speed (and Range) Reading*, David & Charles (Newton Abbot, UK), 2000

Buzan, T. *Use Your Head*, BBC Worldwide (London), 2000

Carney, T. and B. *Liberation Learning: Self-Directed Learning for Students*, Para-Publishing (Windsor, Can), 1988

Chambers, E. and Northedge, A. *The Arts Good Study Guide*, Open University Press (Buckingham, UK), 2000

Clarke, L. and Hawkins, J. *Student Survival Guide*, How To Books (Oxford, UK), 2001

Deese, J. *How to Study*, McGraw-Hill (New York), 1969

Ellis, D.B. *Becoming a Master Student*, College Survival (Rapid City, US), 1993

Hanau, L. *The Study Game*, Barnes & Noble (New York), 1979

Hennessy, B. *Writing an Essay*, How To Books (Oxford, UK), 2000

Jones, B. and Johnson, R. *Making the Grade*, Manchester University Press (Manchester, UK), 1990

Lane, A., Northedge, A., Peasgood, A. and Thomas, J. *The Sciences Good Study Guide*, Open University Press (Milton Keynes, UK), 2002

MacFarlane, P. and Hodson, S. *Studying Effectively and Efficiently: An Integrated System*, University of Toronto (Toronto), 1983

Nilsson, V. *Improve Your Study Skills*, Athabasca University (Athabasca, Can), 1989

Northedge, A. *The Good Study Guide*, Open University Press (Milton Keynes, UK), 2002

Pauk, W. *How to Study in College*, Houghton Mifflin (Boston, US), 1984

Robertson, H. *Bridge to College Success*, Heinle & Heinle Publishers (Boston, US), 1991

Tracy, E. *The Student's Guide to Exam Success*, Open University Press (Buckingham, UK), 2002

University of British Columbia, *Strategies for Studying*, Orca (Victoria, Can), 1996

Walter, T. and Siebert, A. *Student Success*, Holt Reinhart and Winston (New York) 1987

Wong, L. *Essential Study Skills*, Houghton Mifflin (Boston), 1999

Dominic O'Brien is renowned for his phenomenal feats of memory and for outwitting the casinos of Las Vegas at the blackjack tables, eventually resulting in a ban. In addition to winning the World Memory Championships eight times, he was named Brain of the Year in 1994 and Grandmaster of Memory by the Brain Trust of Great Britain in 1995. He has made numerous appearances on TV and radio and holds a host of world records, including one for memorizing 2,385 random binary digits in 30 minutes. He is author of the bestseller *You Can Have an Amazing Memory, Learn to Remember* and *How to Develop a Brilliant Memory Week by Week.*